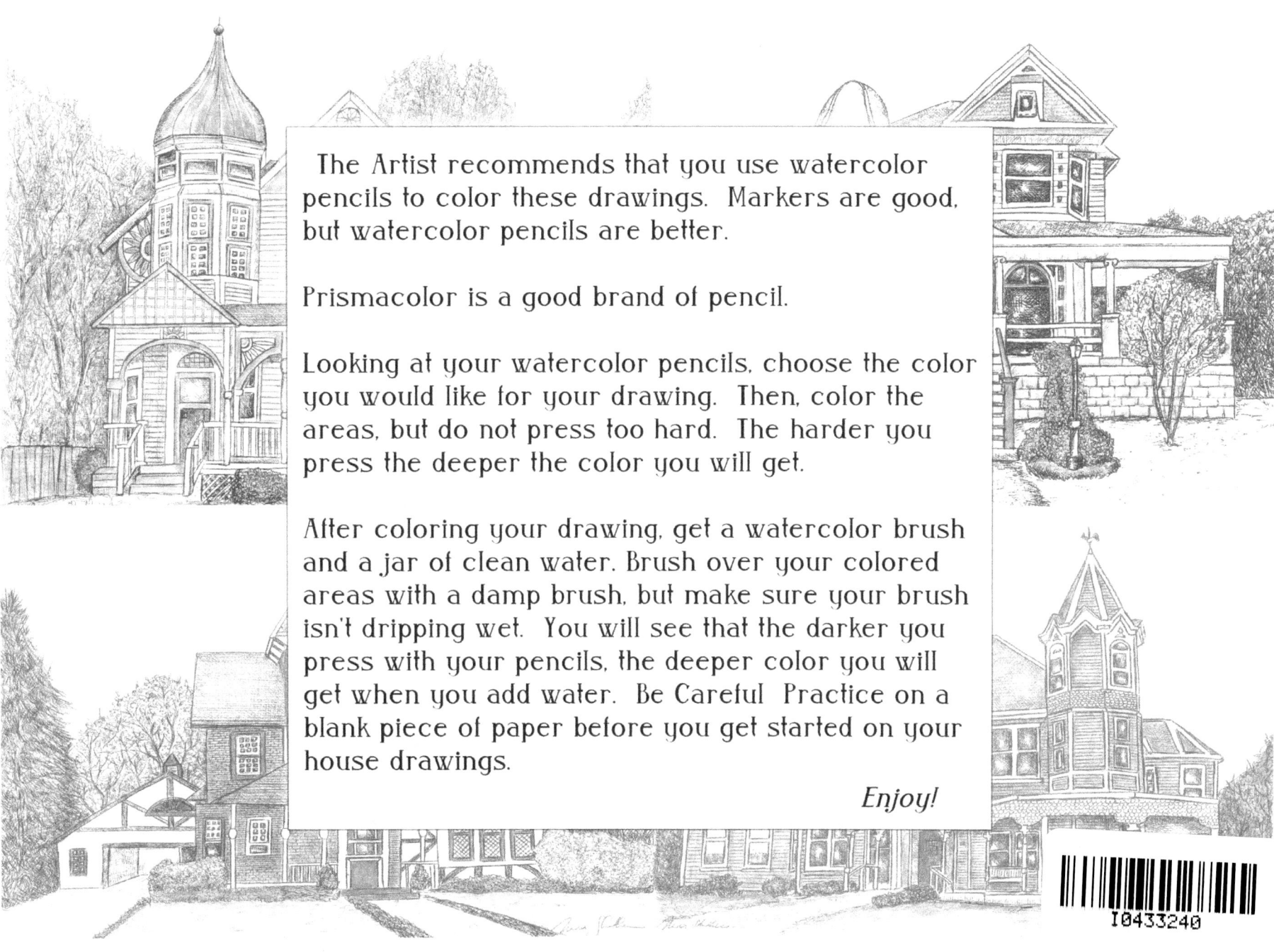

The Artist recommends that you use watercolor pencils to color these drawings. Markers are good, but watercolor pencils are better.

Prismacolor is a good brand of pencil.

Looking at your watercolor pencils, choose the color you would like for your drawing. Then, color the areas, but do not press too hard. The harder you press the deeper the color you will get.

After coloring your drawing, get a watercolor brush and a jar of clean water. Brush over your colored areas with a damp brush, but make sure your brush isn't dripping wet. You will see that the darker you press with your pencils, the deeper color you will get when you add water. Be Careful Practice on a blank piece of paper before you get started on your house drawings.

Enjoy!

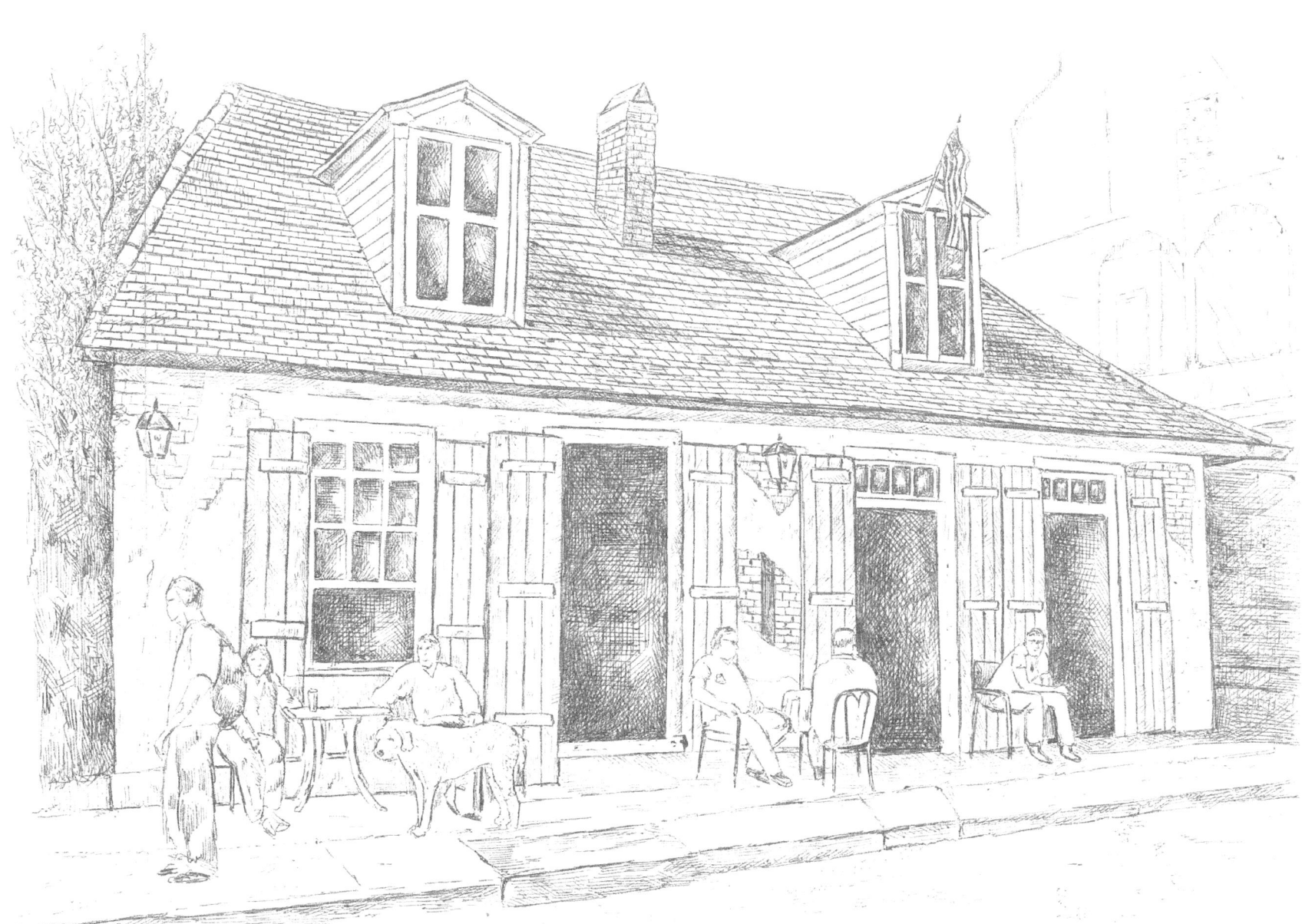

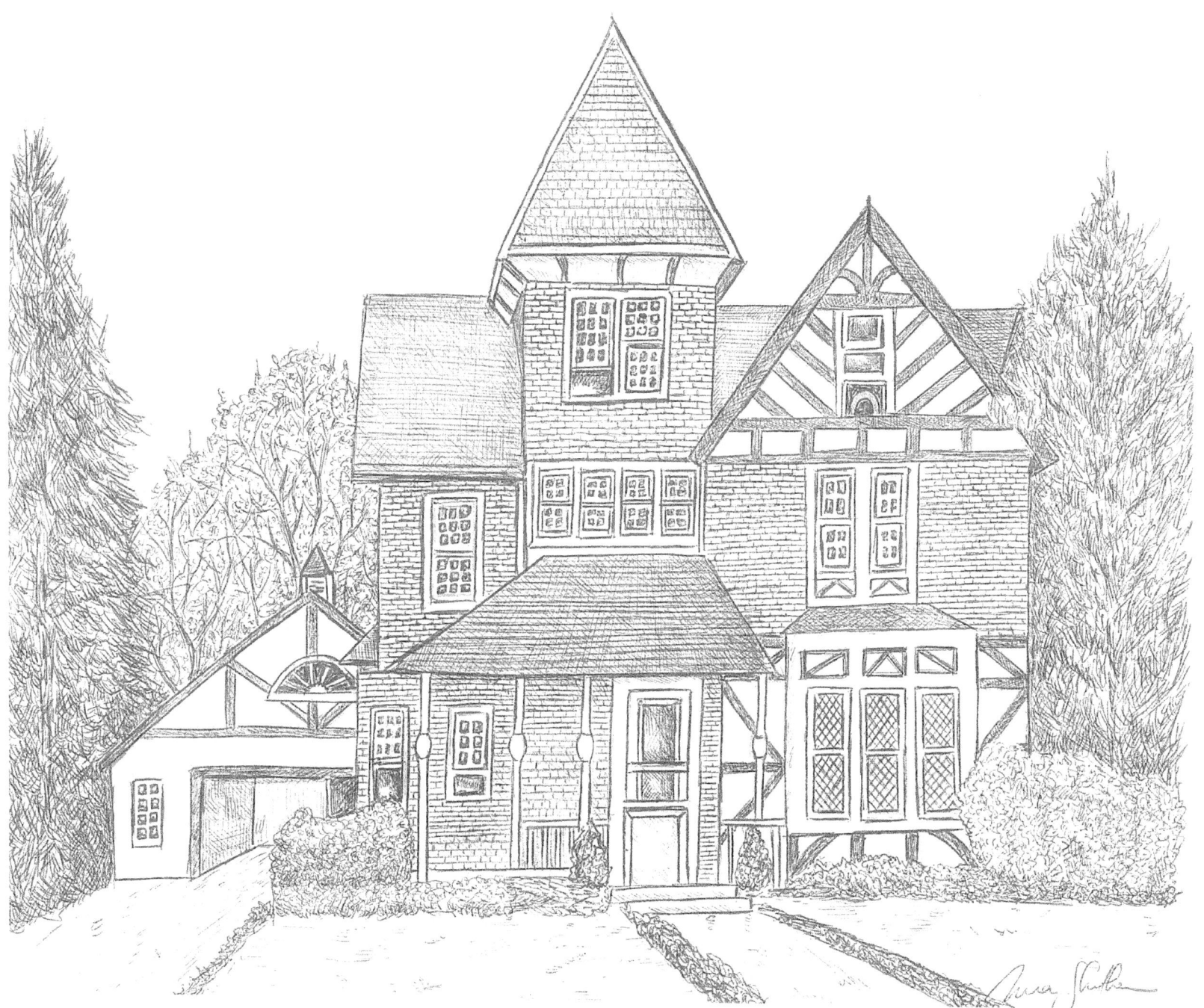

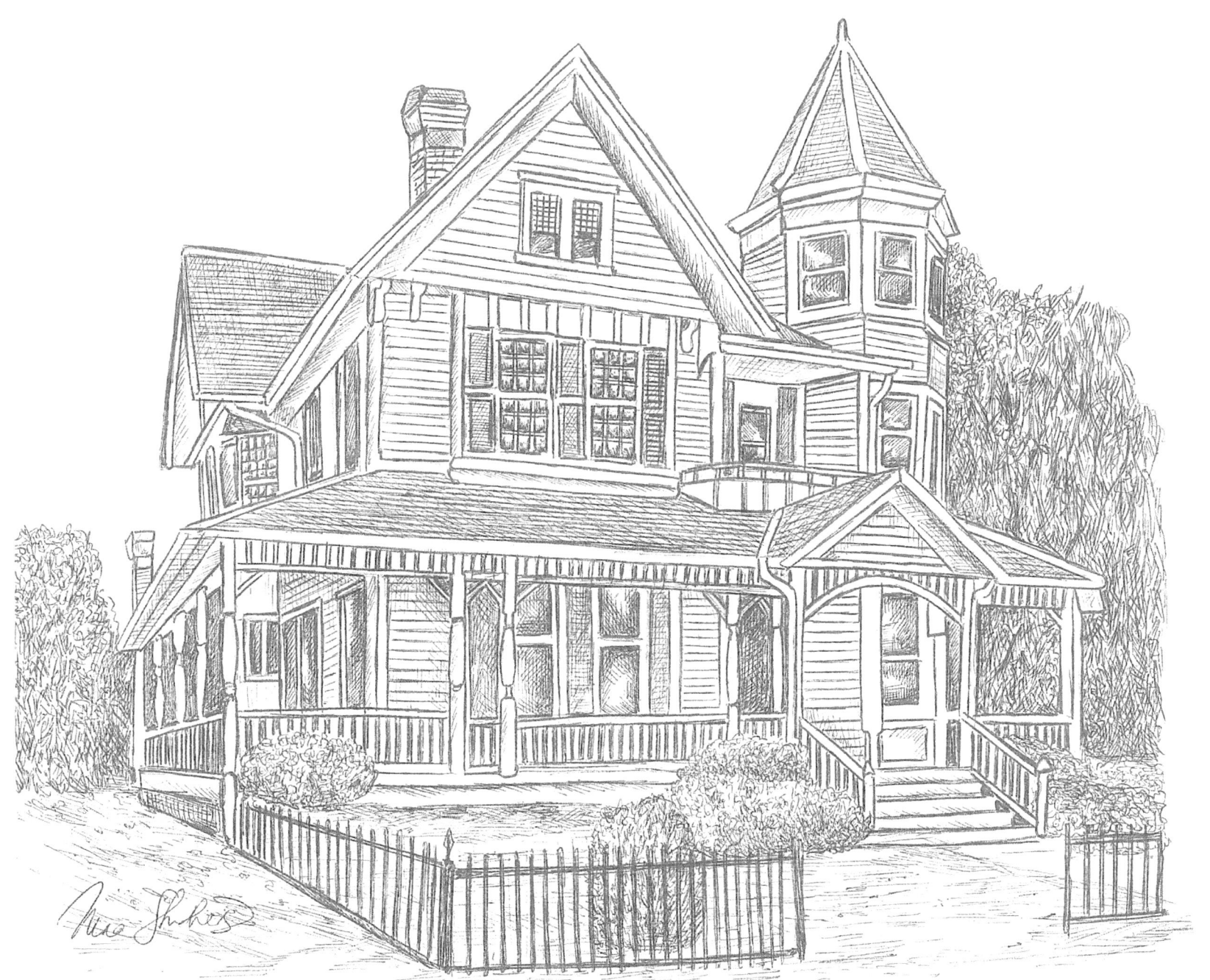

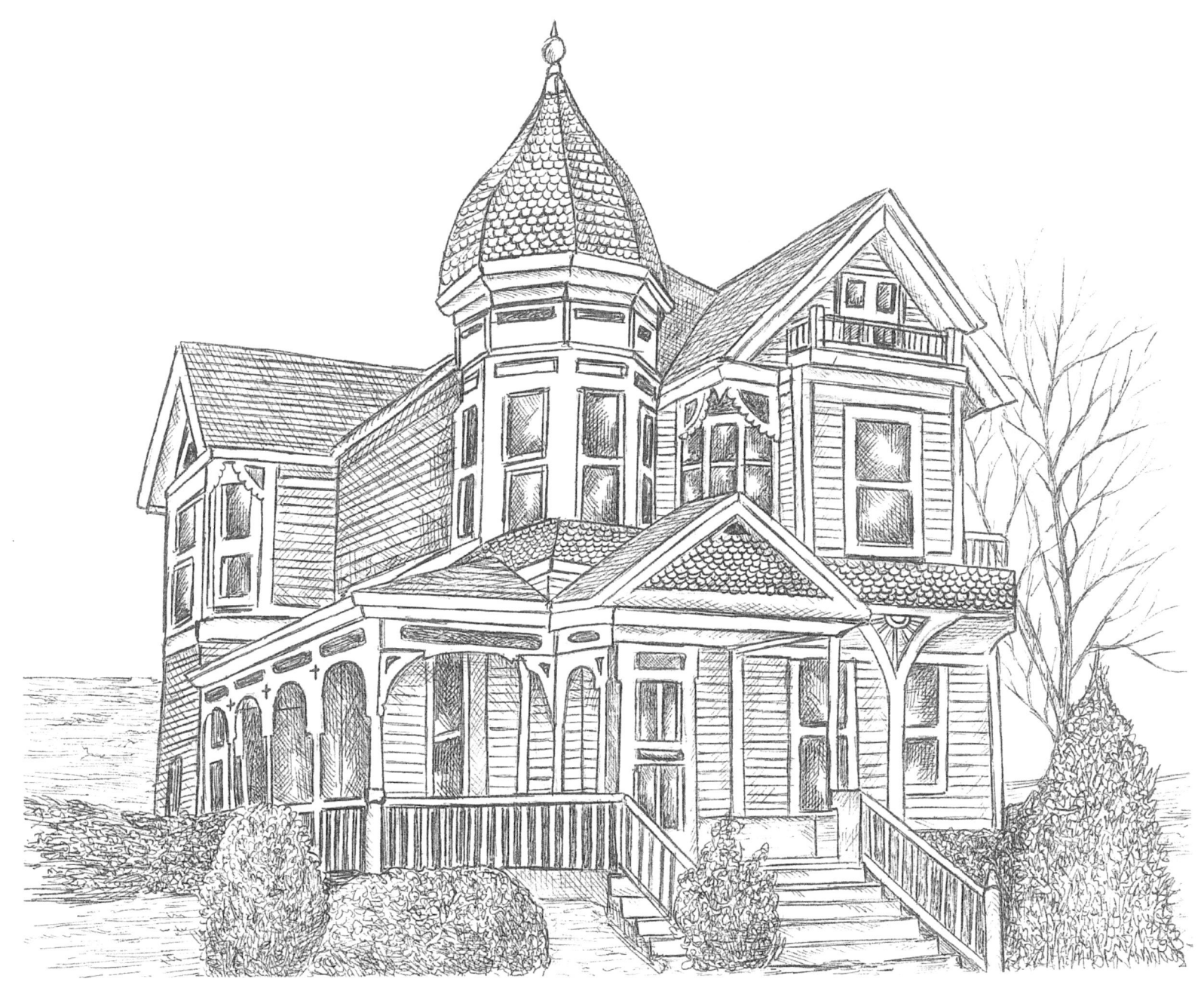

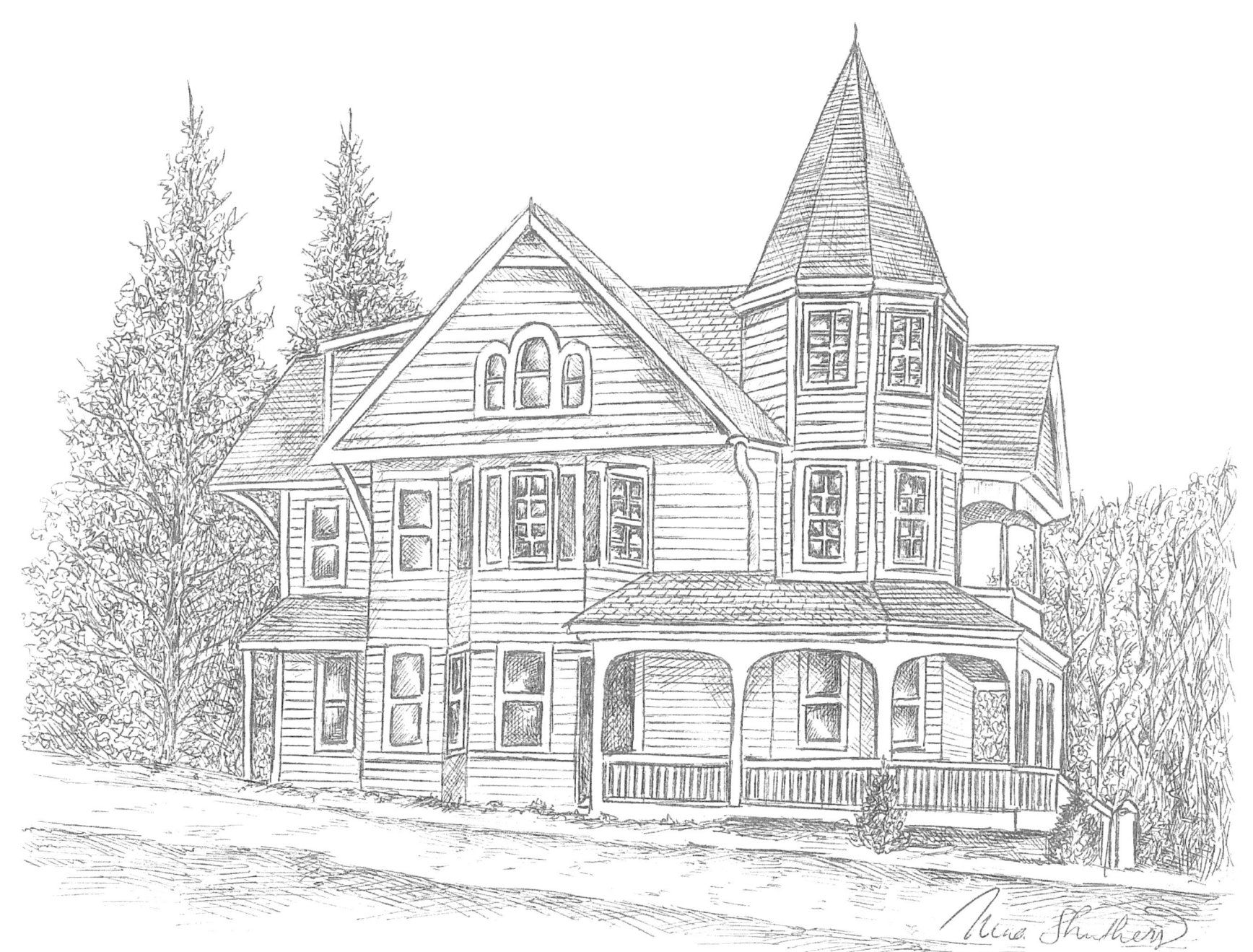

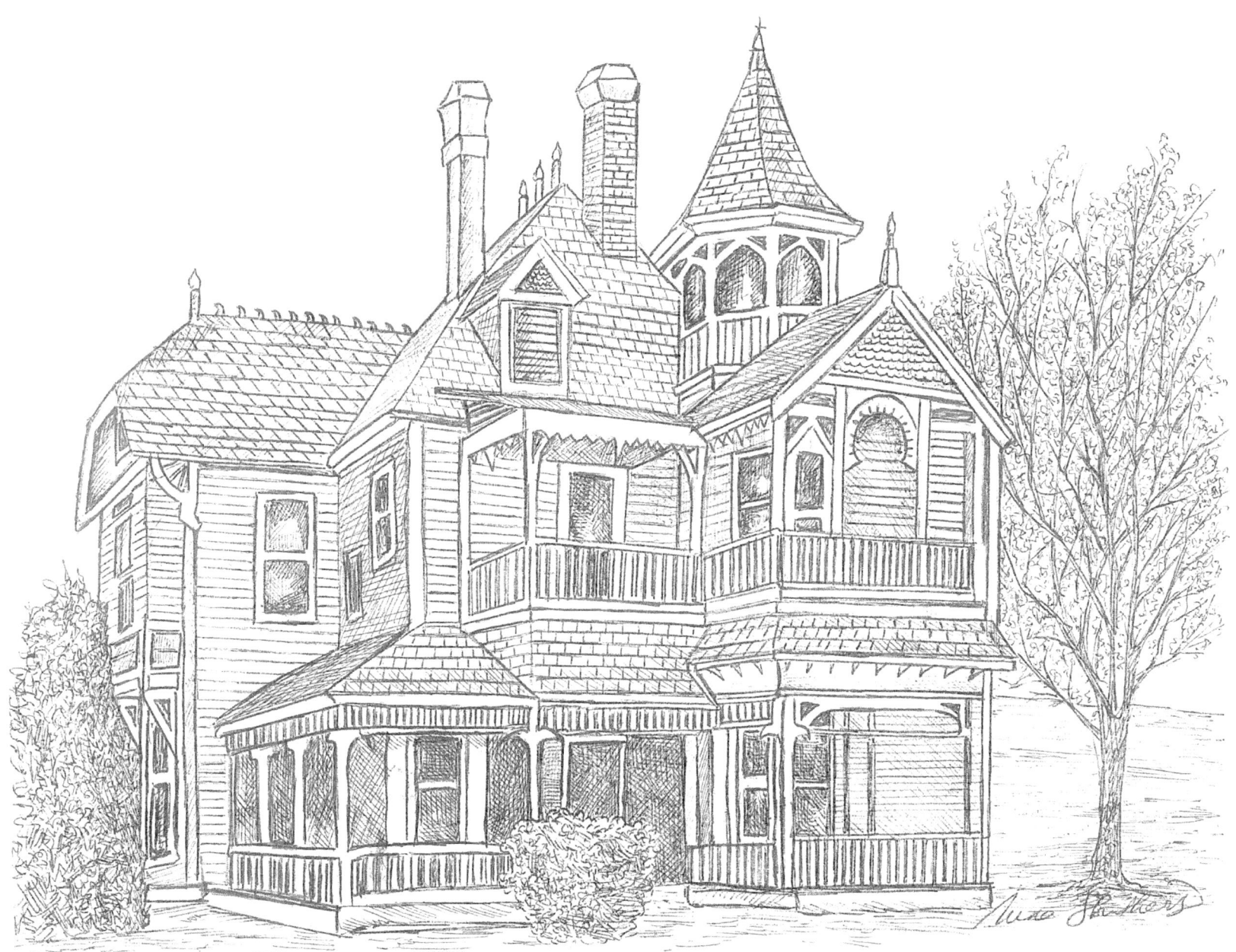

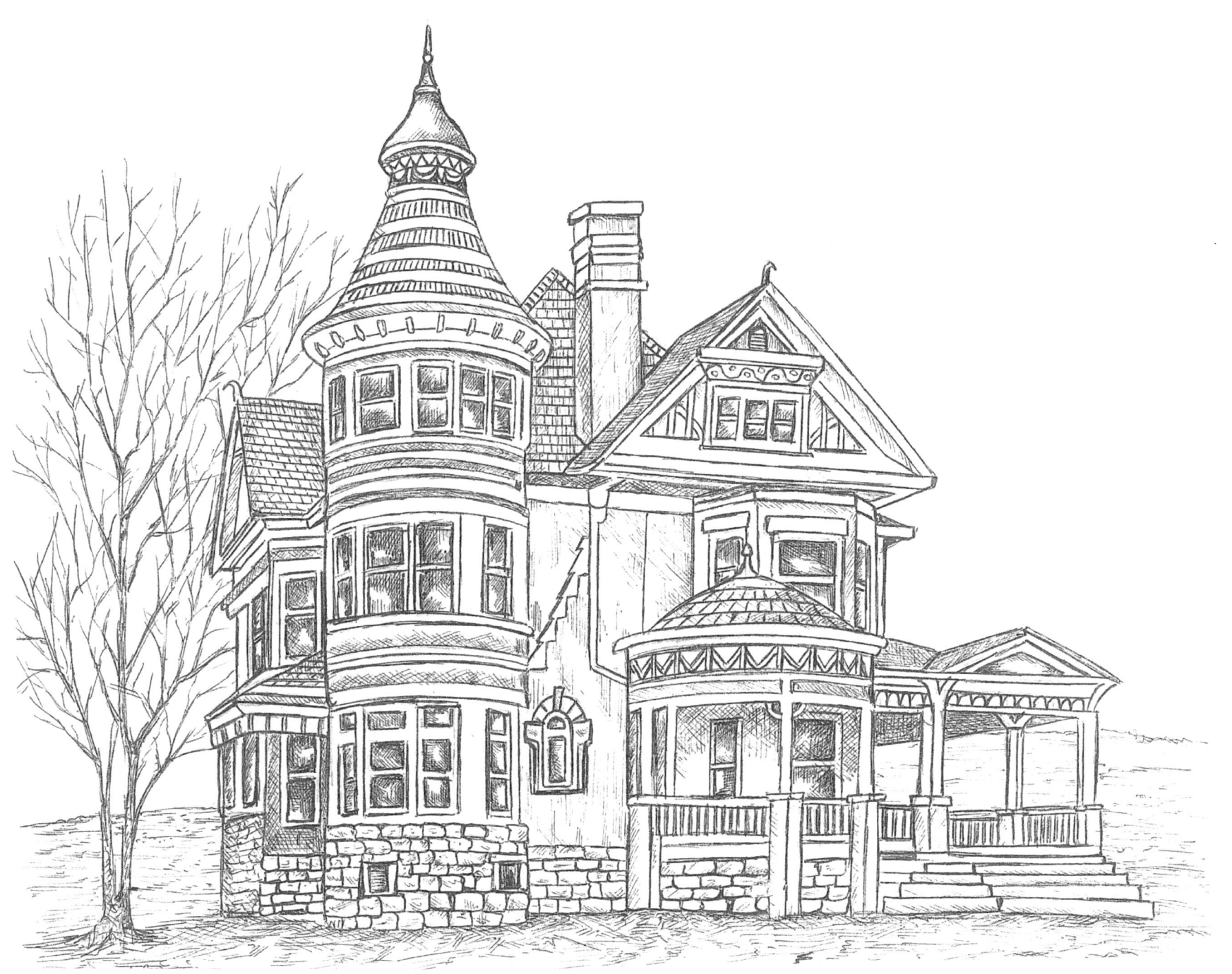

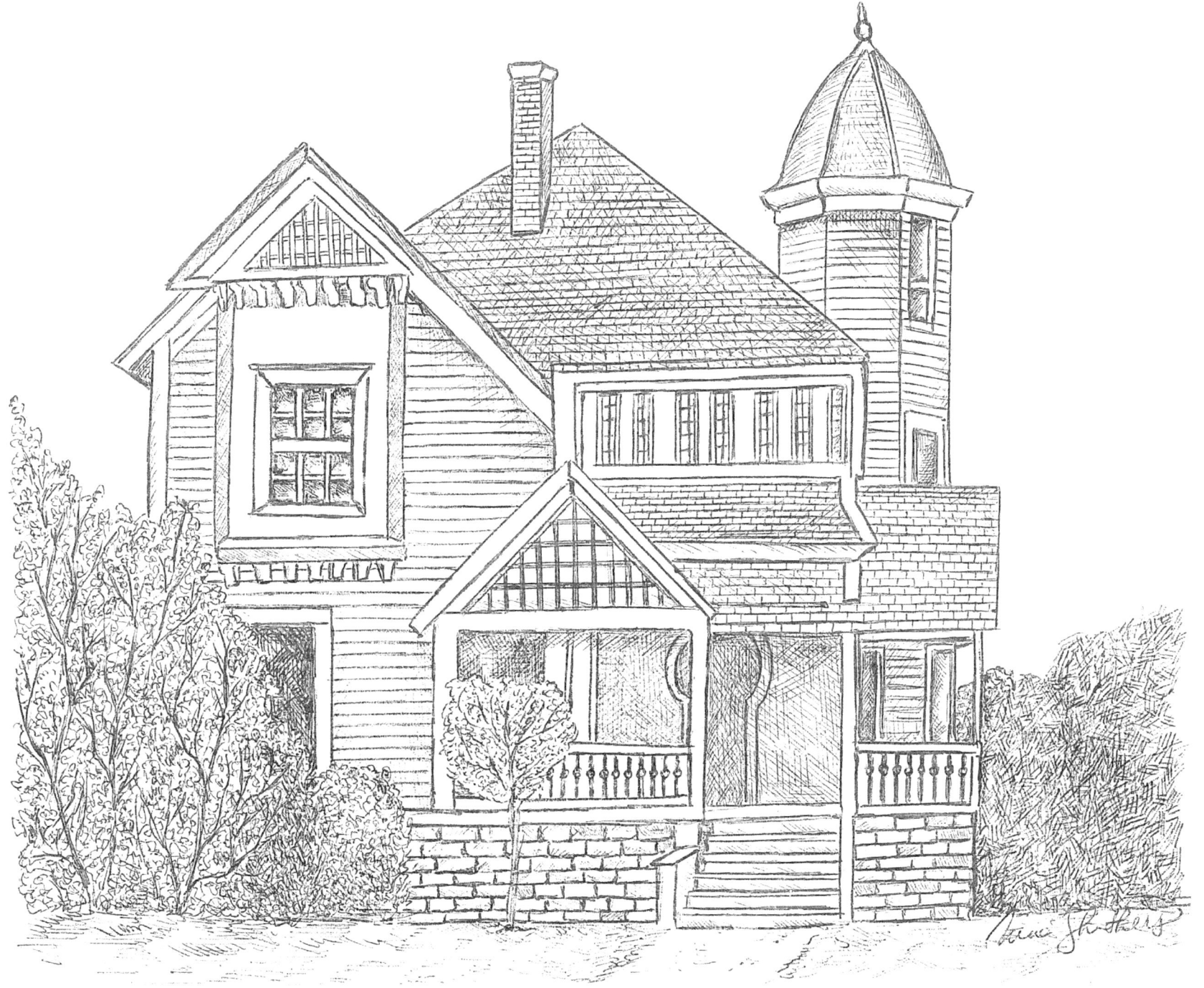

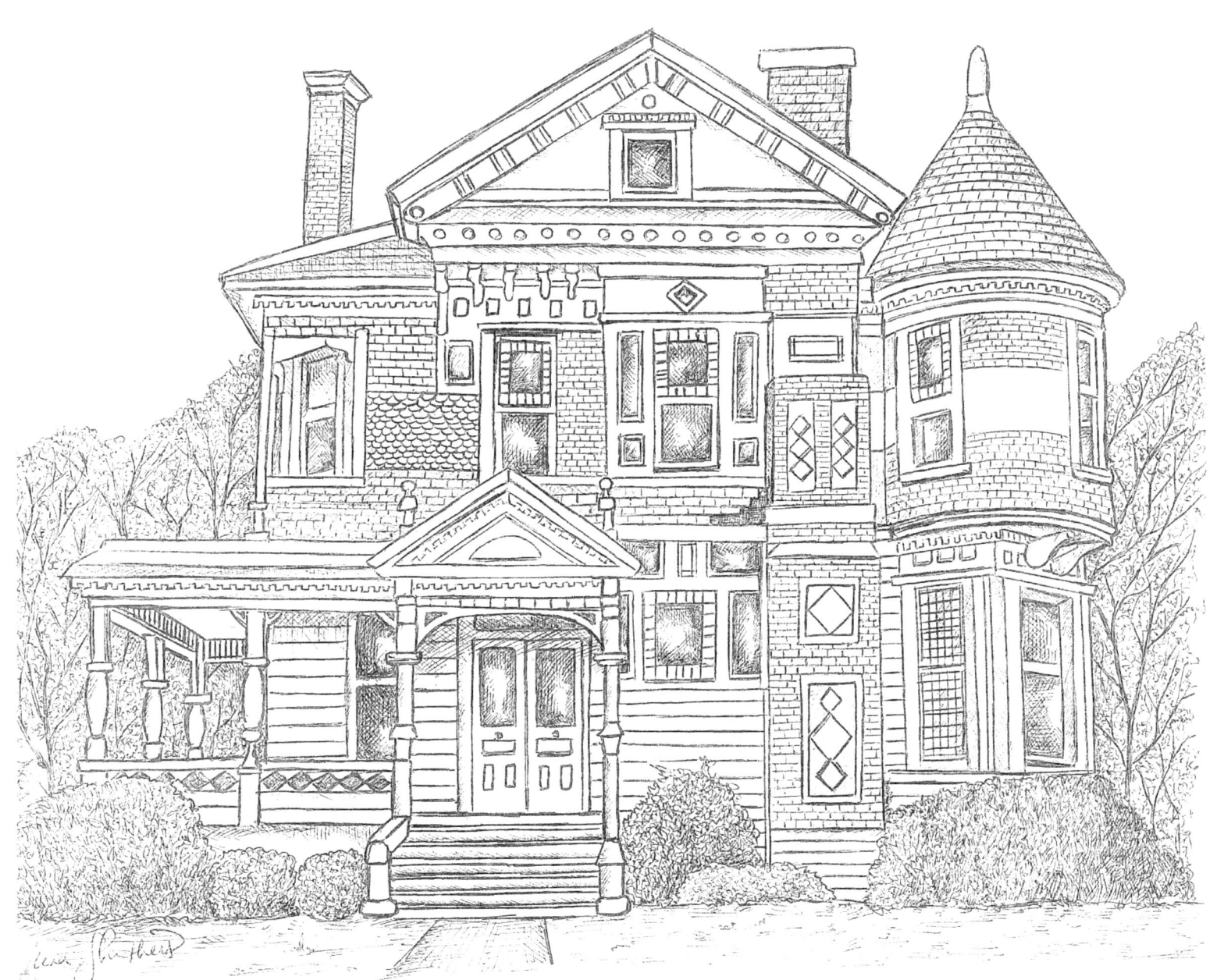

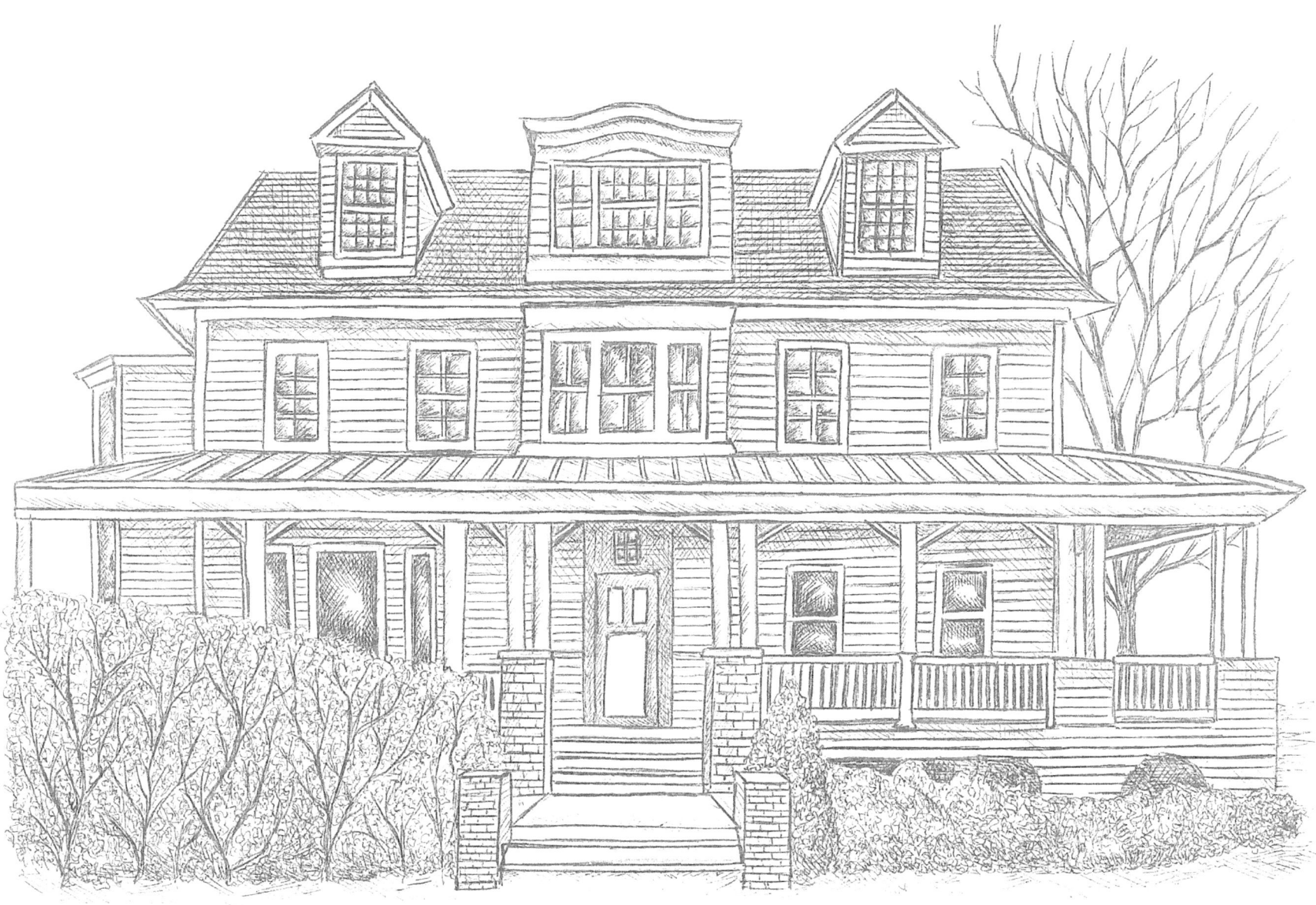

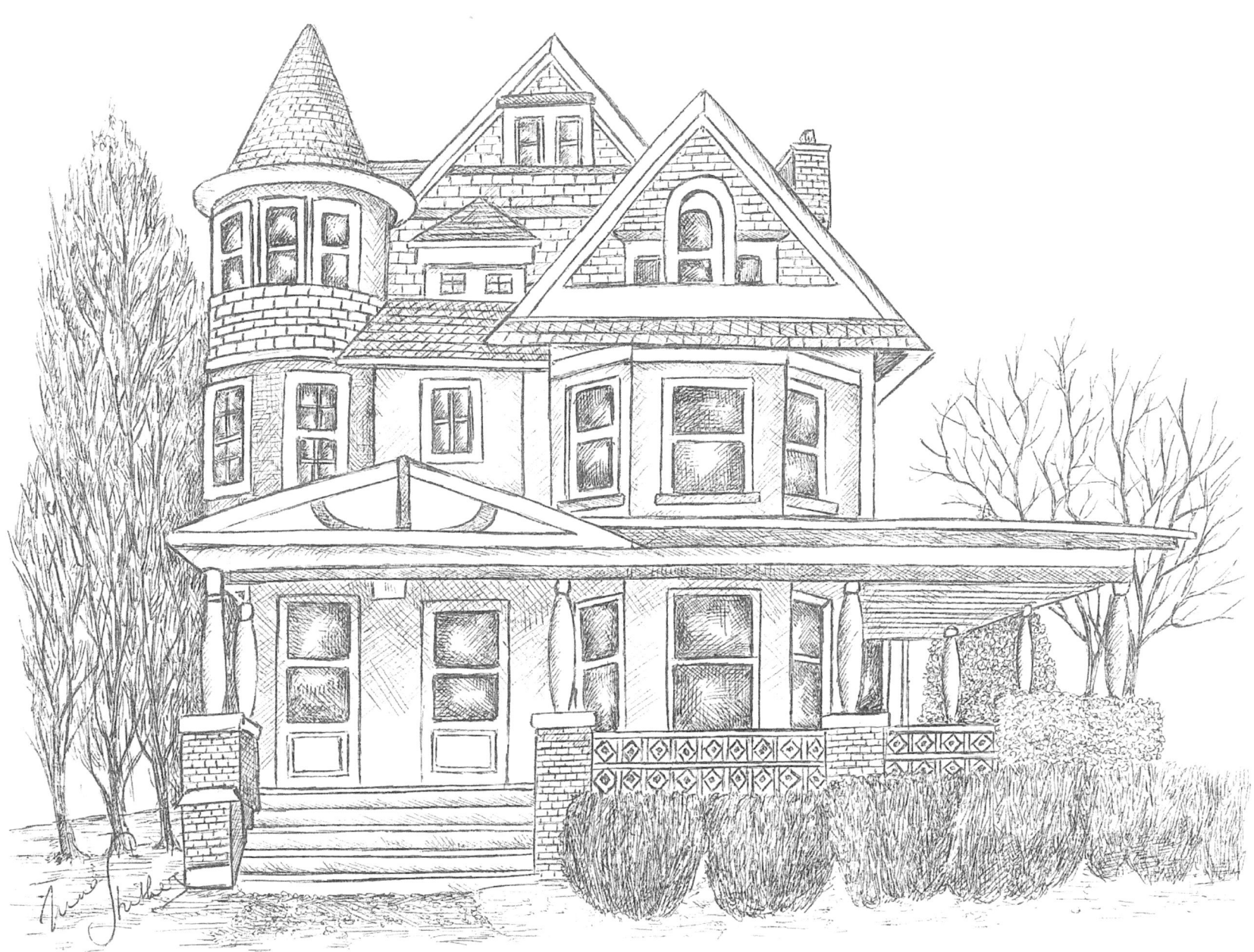

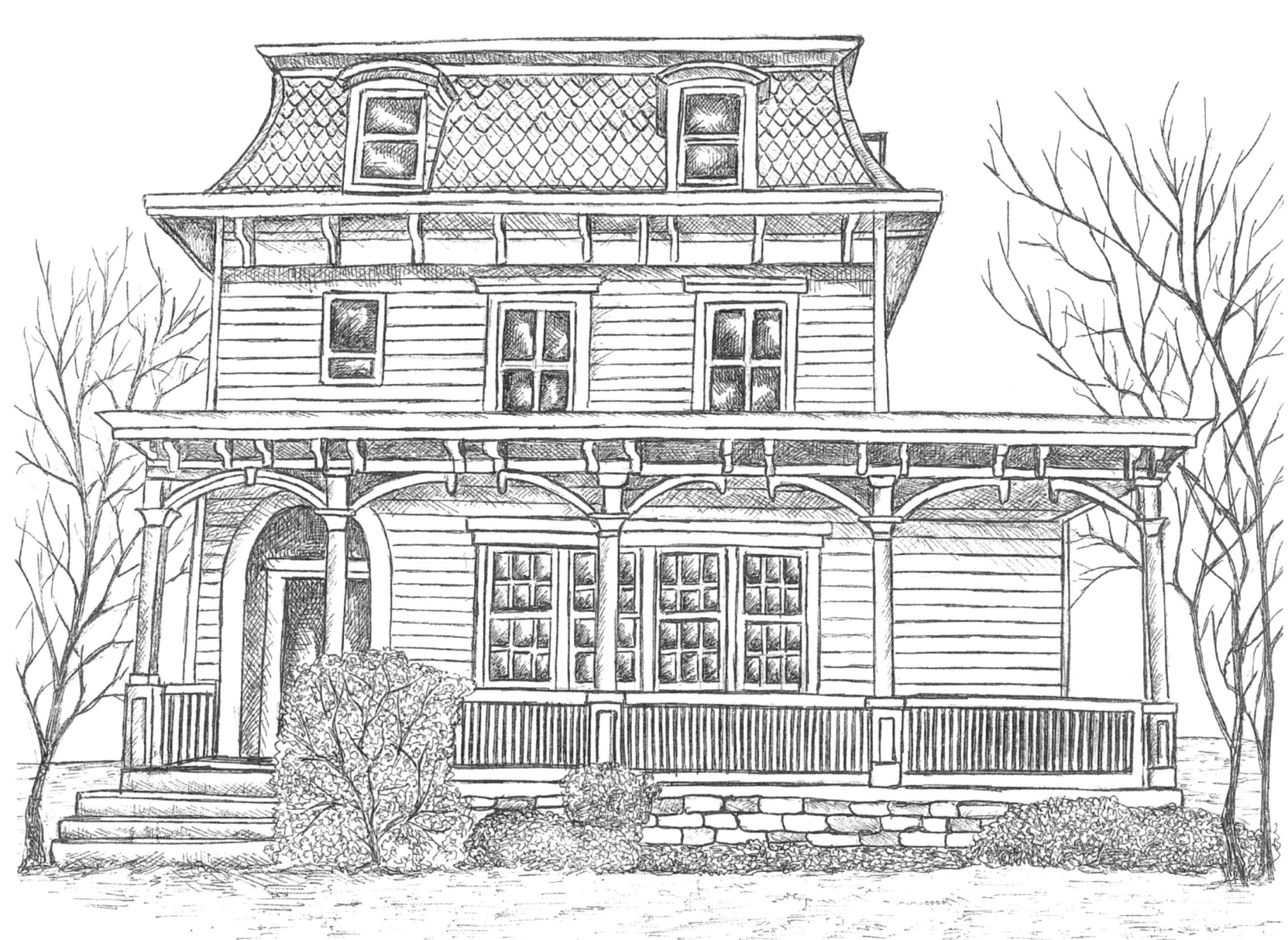

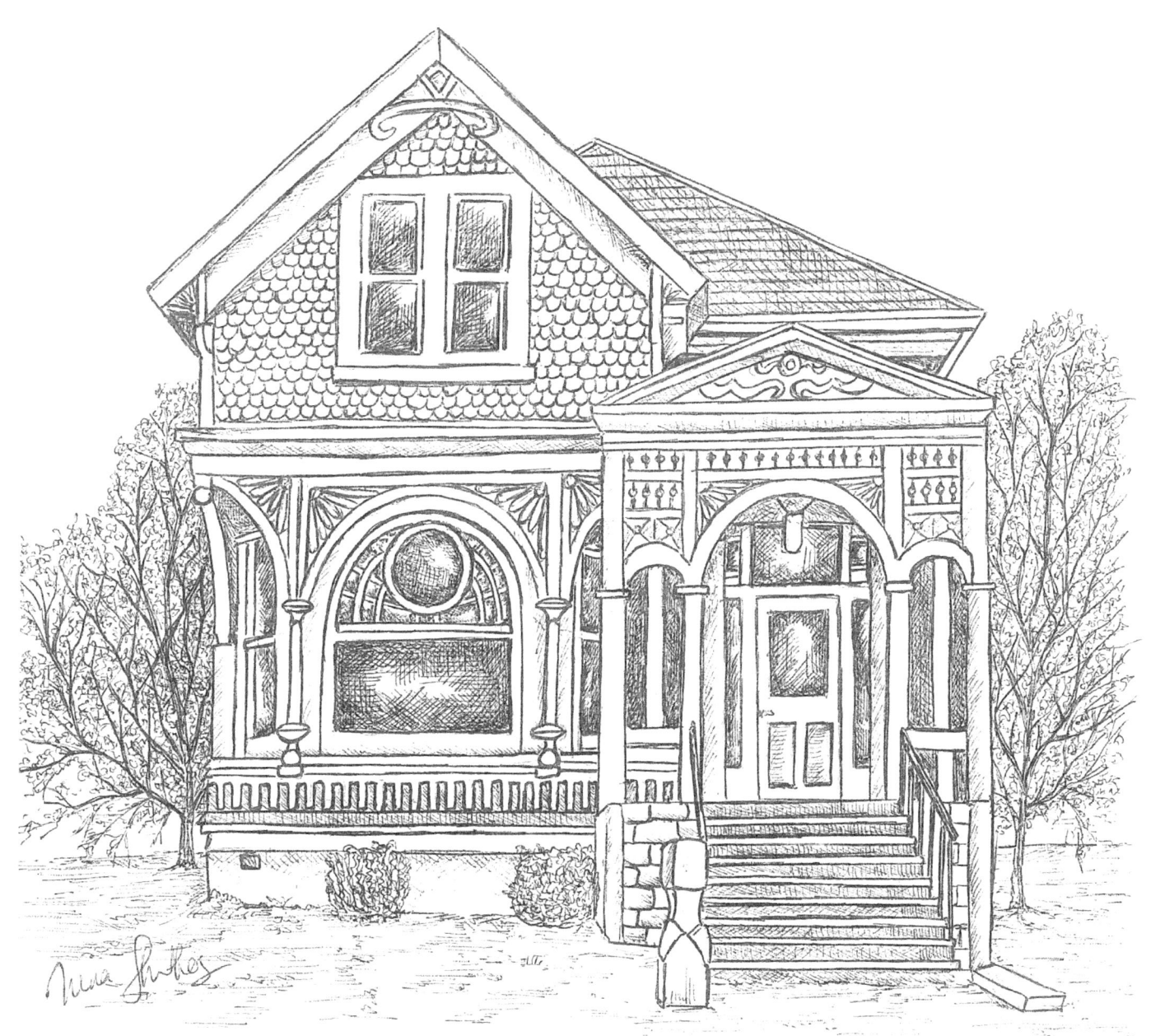

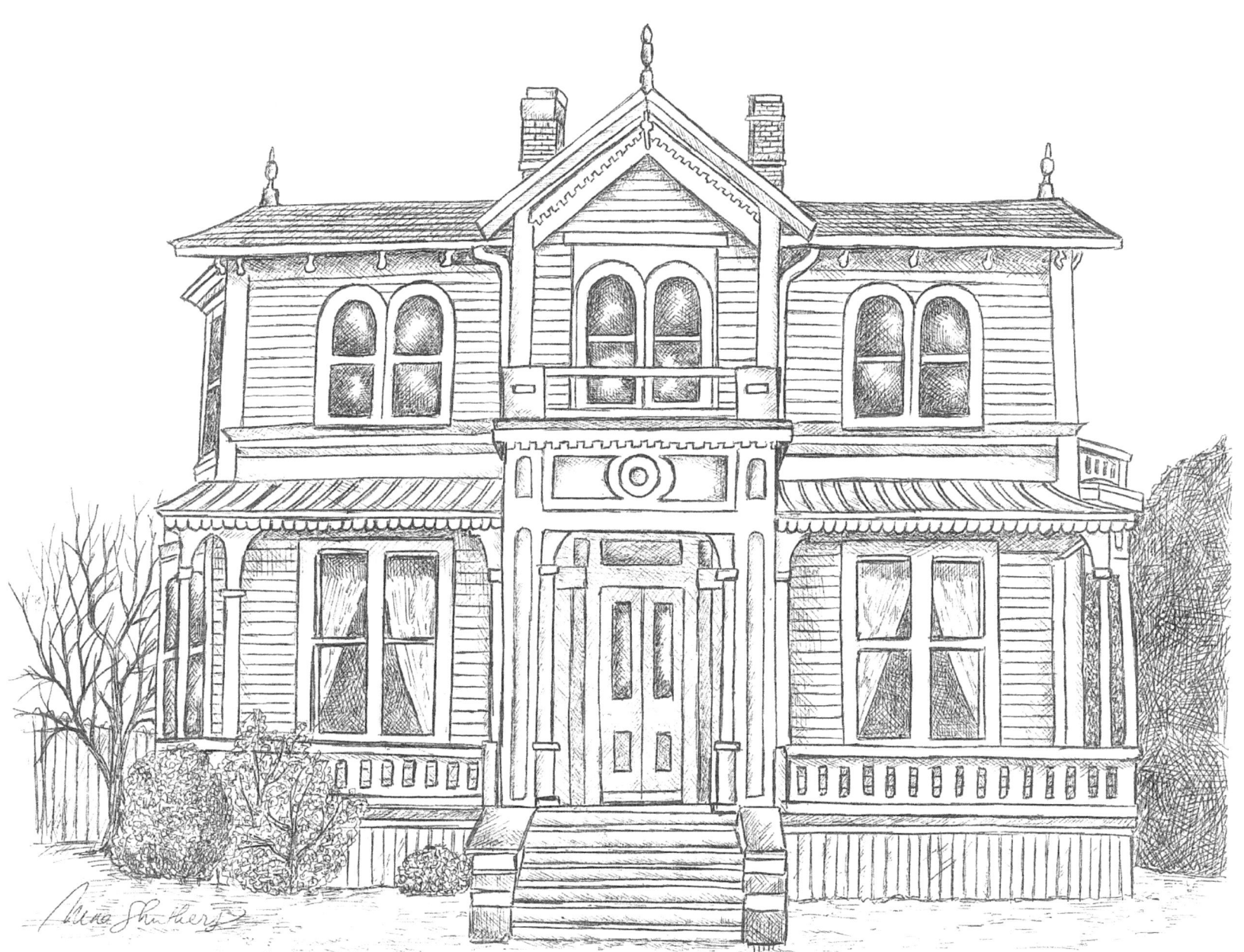

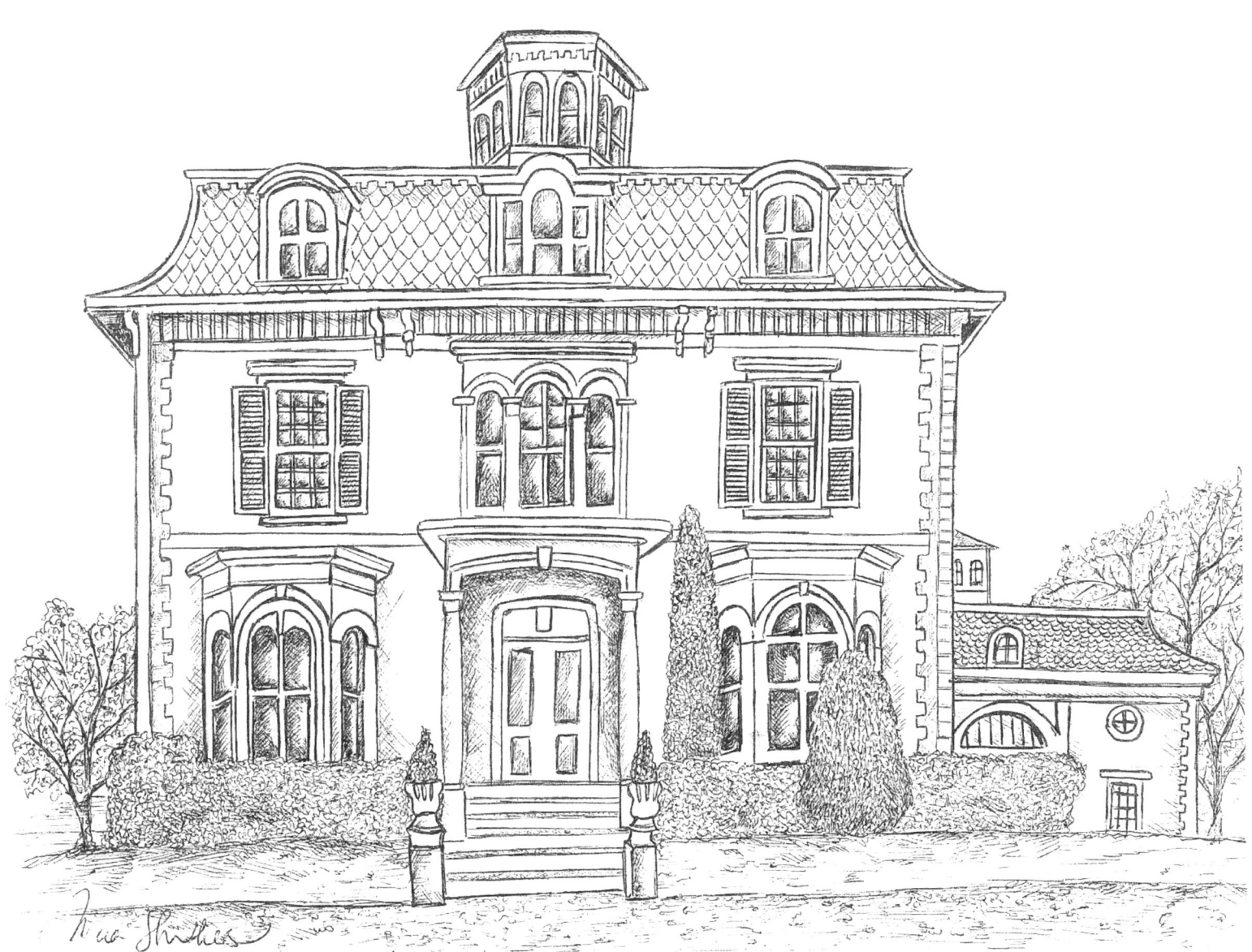

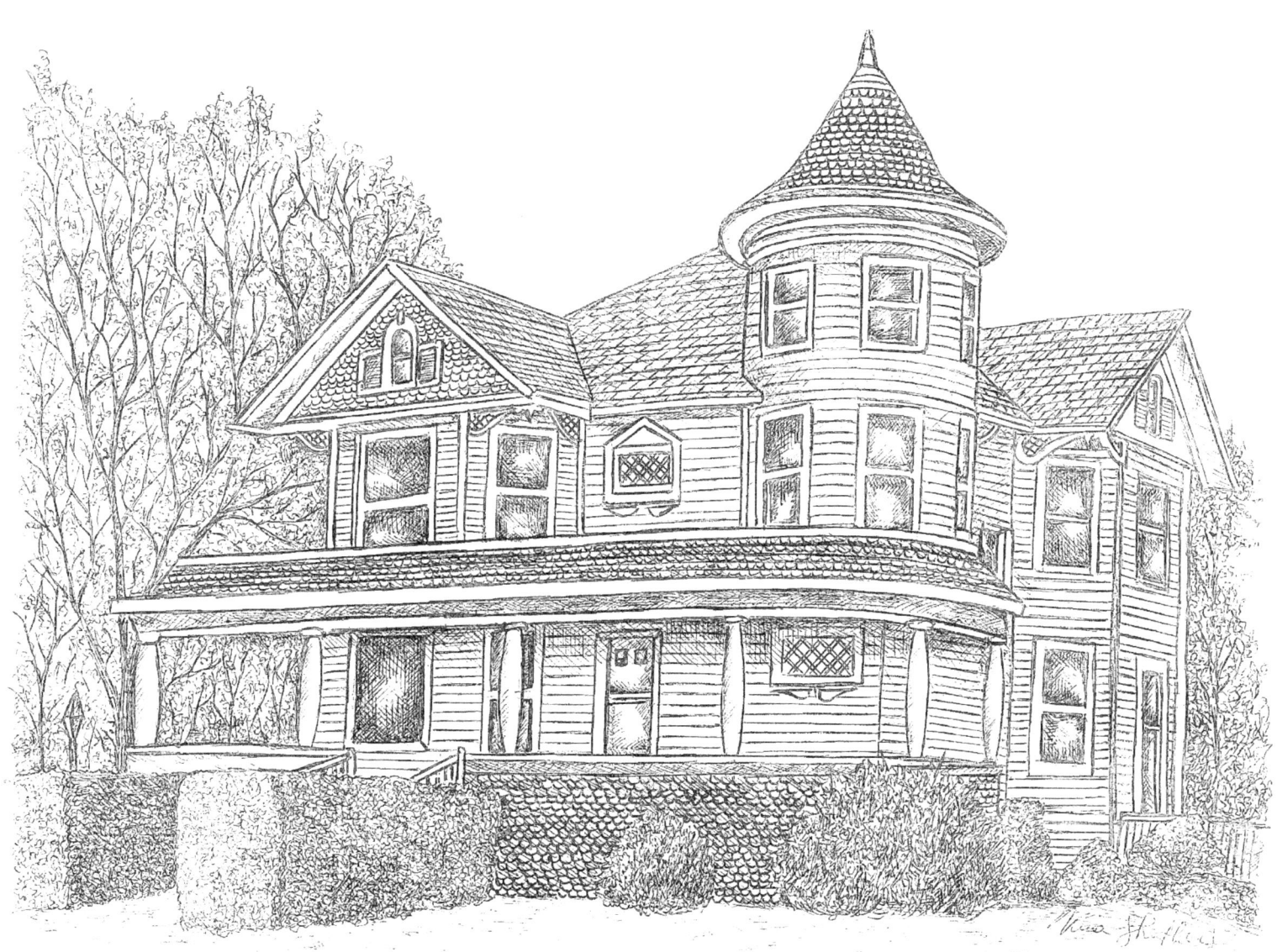

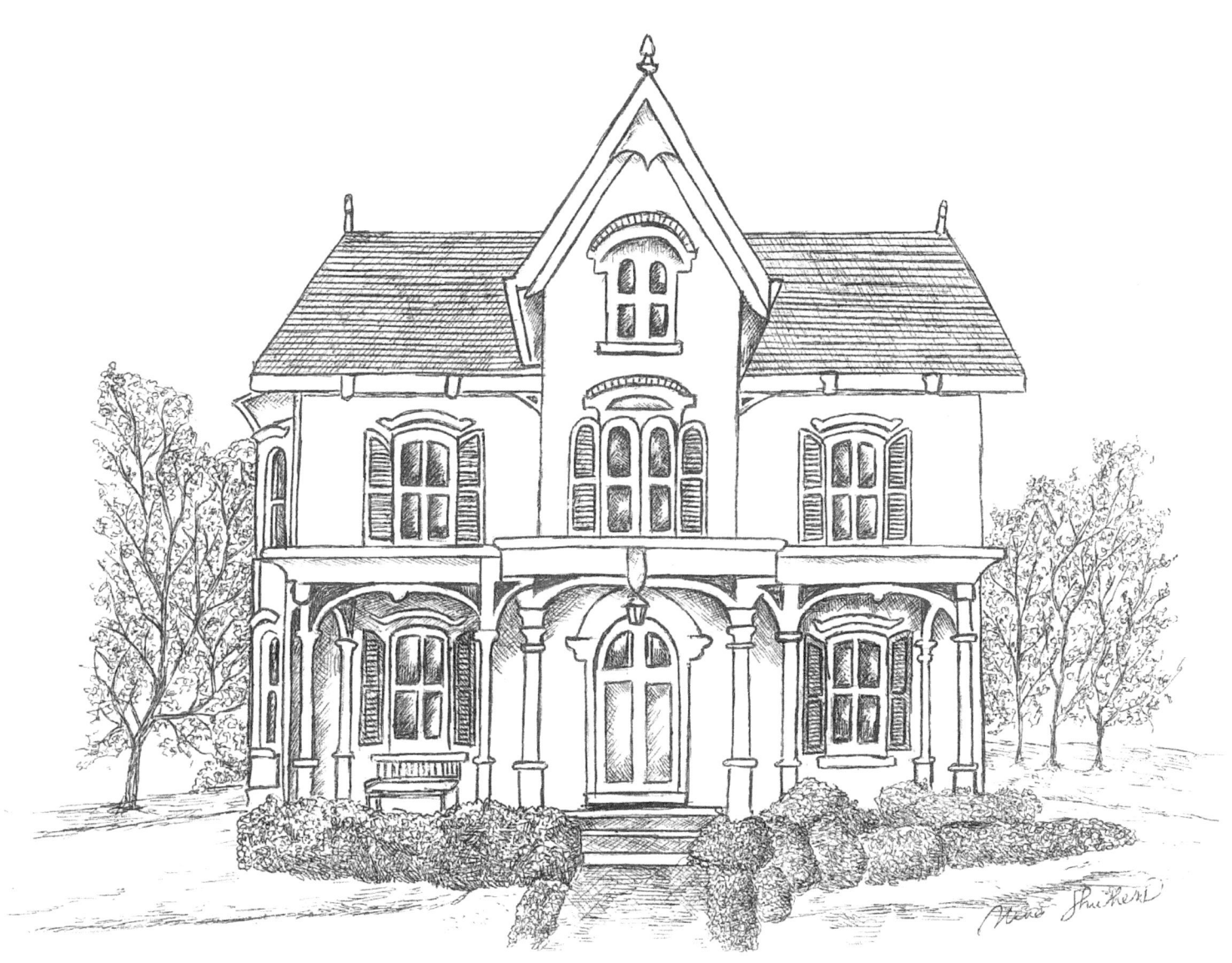

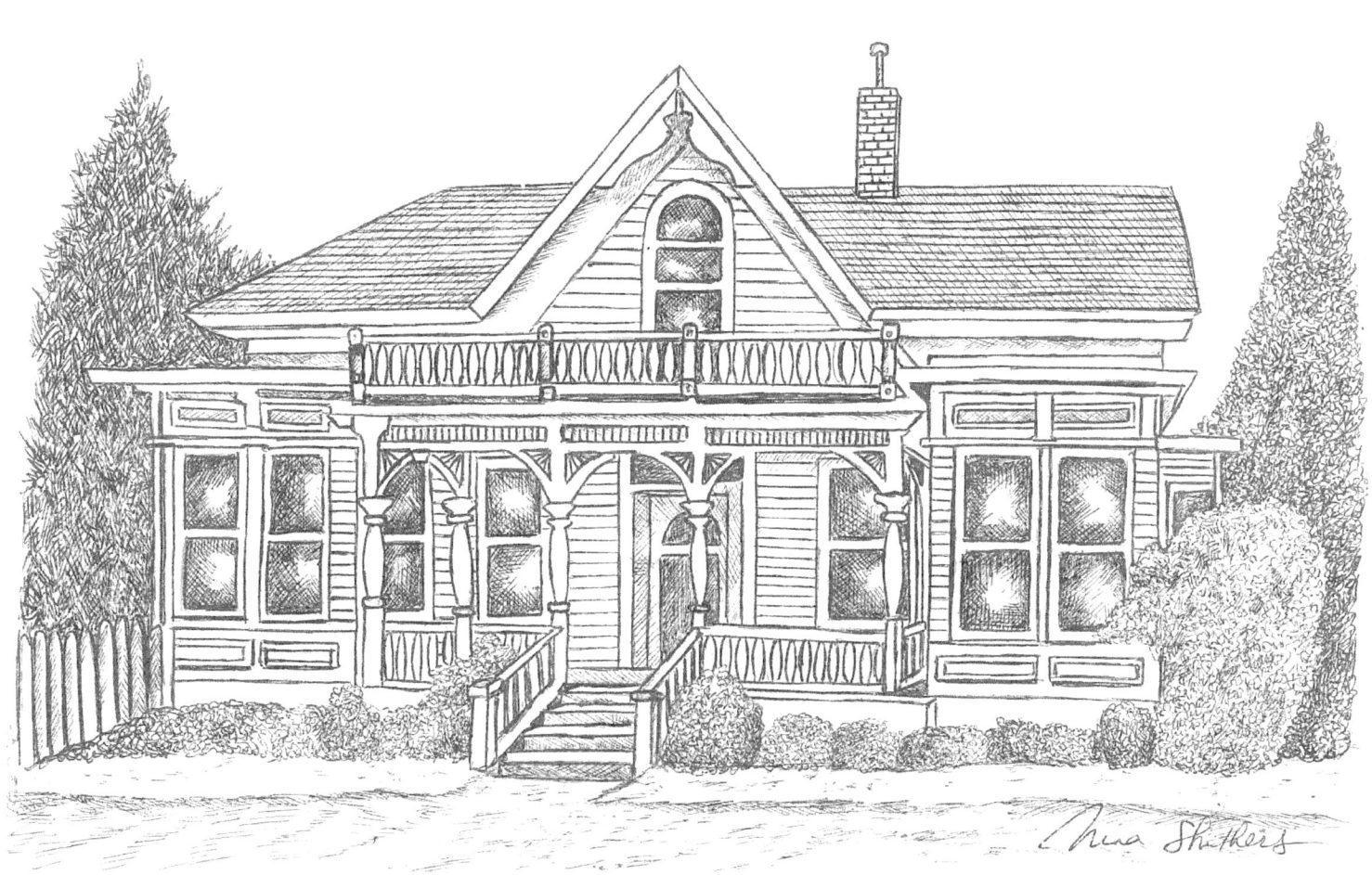

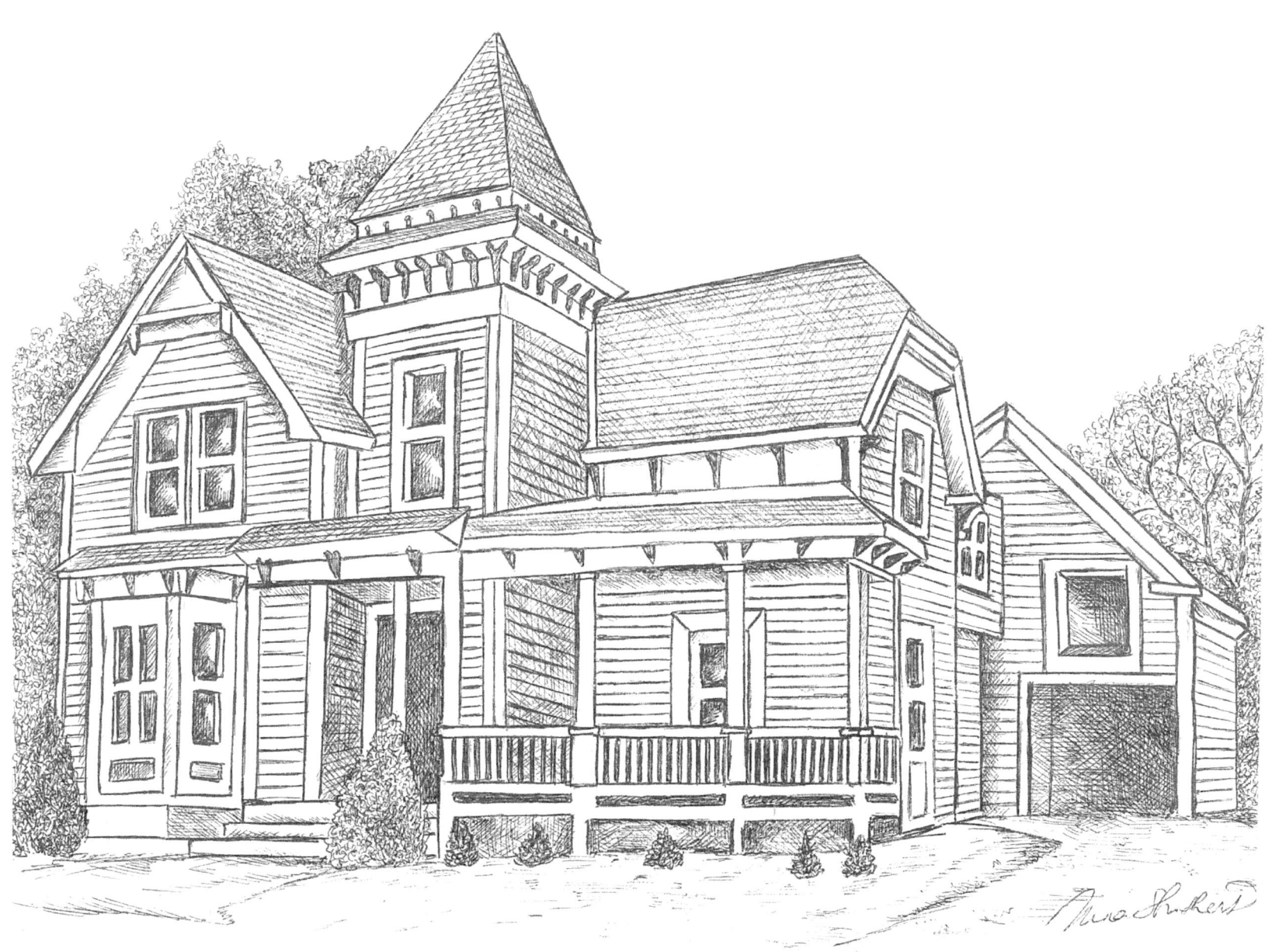

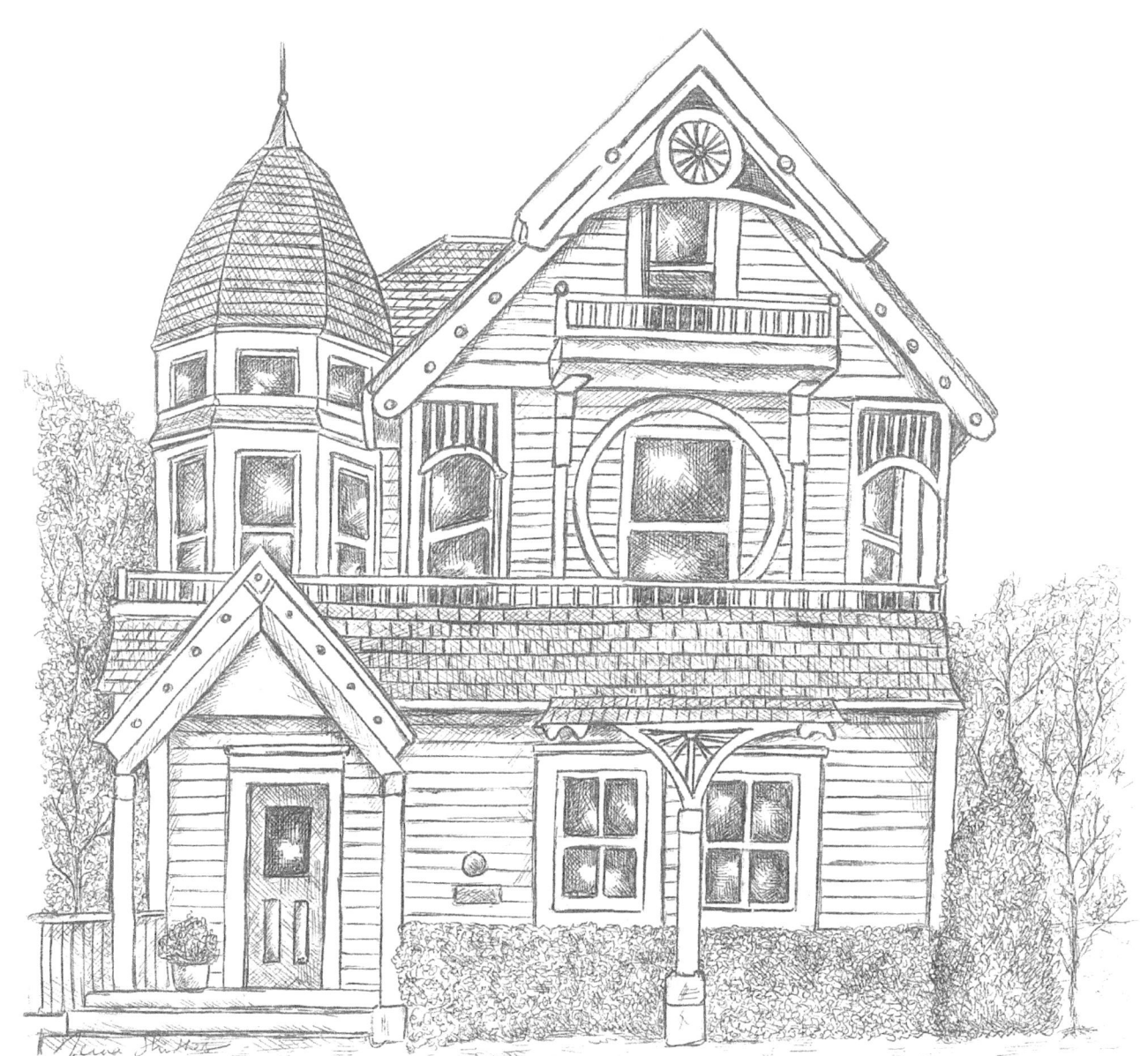

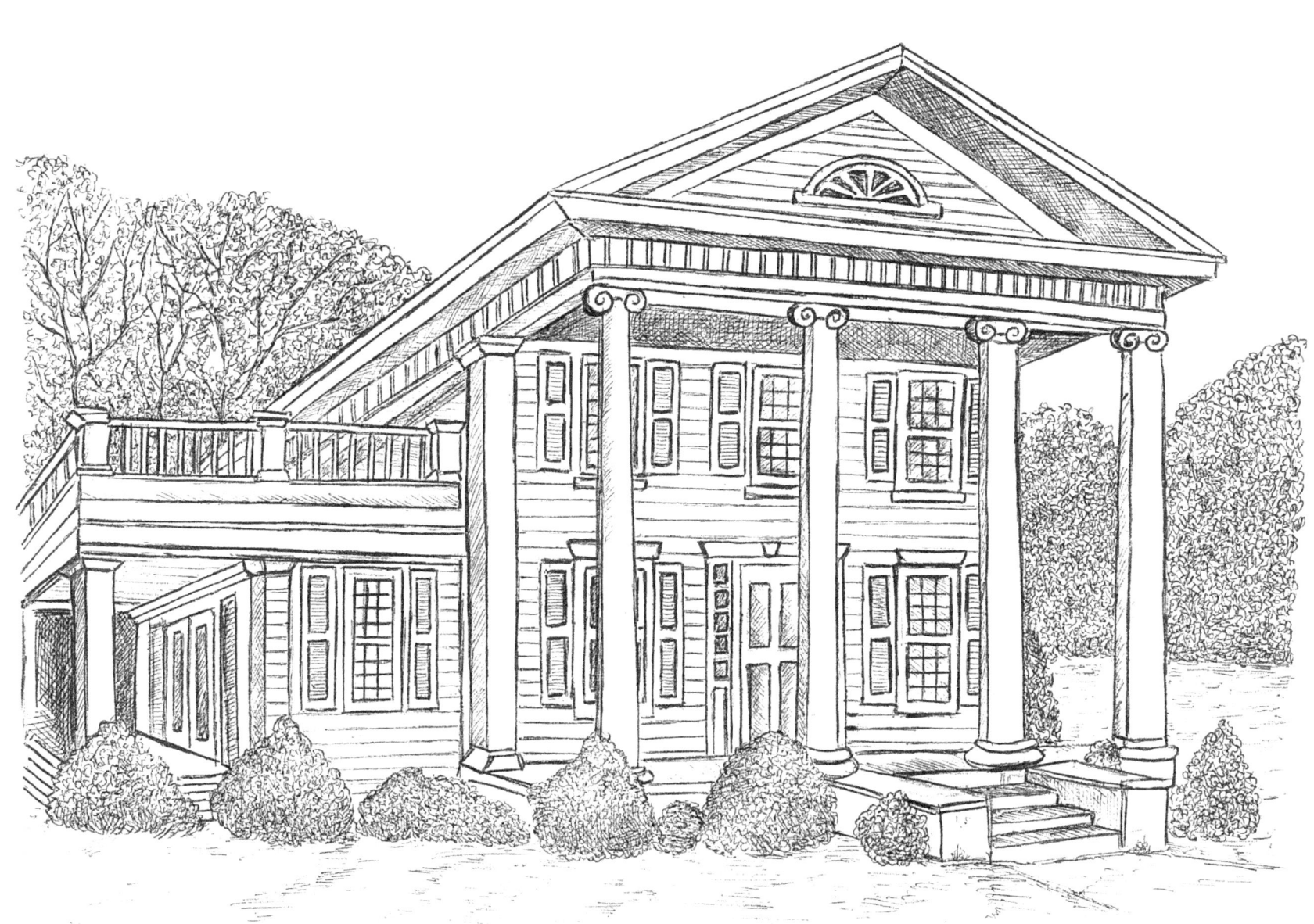

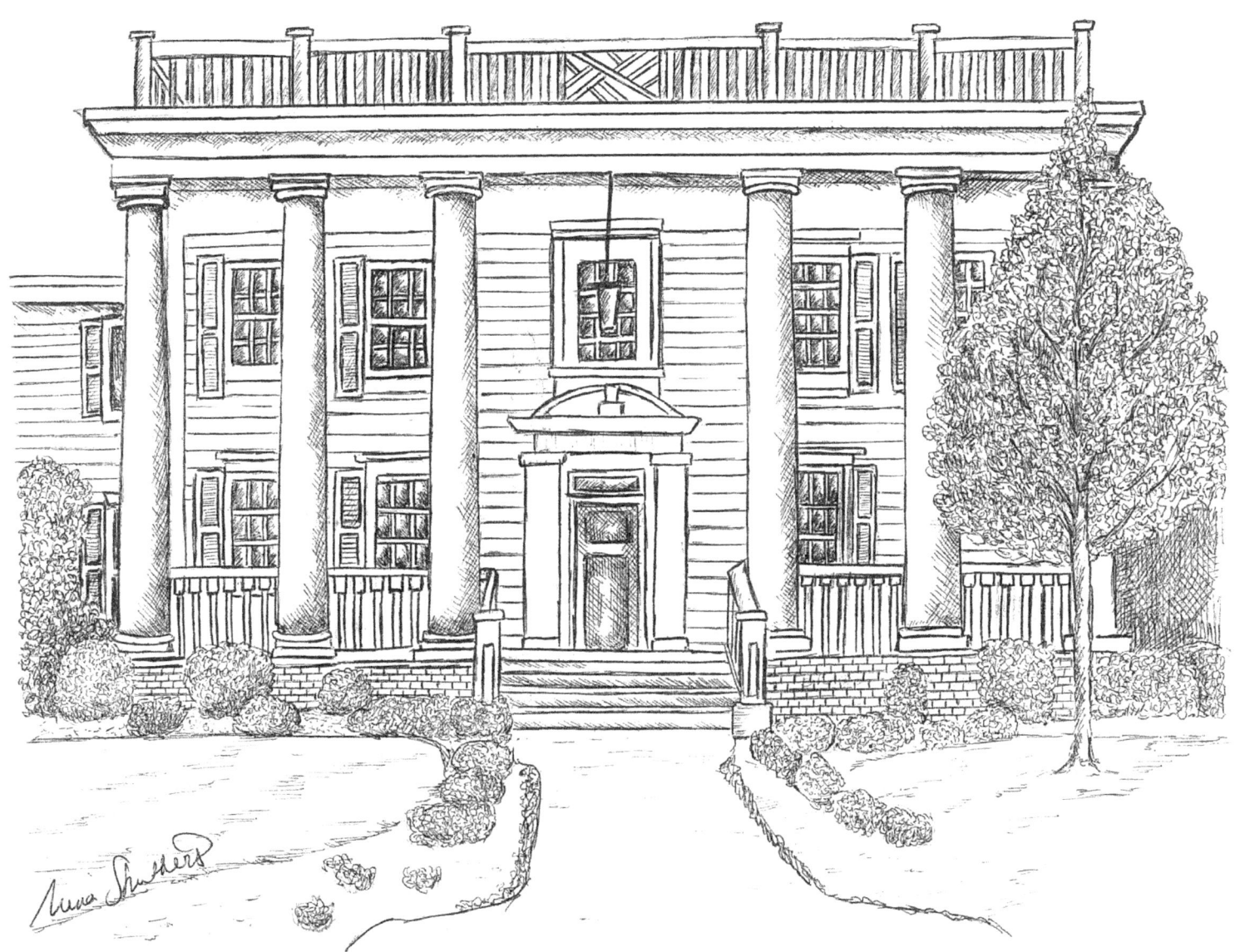

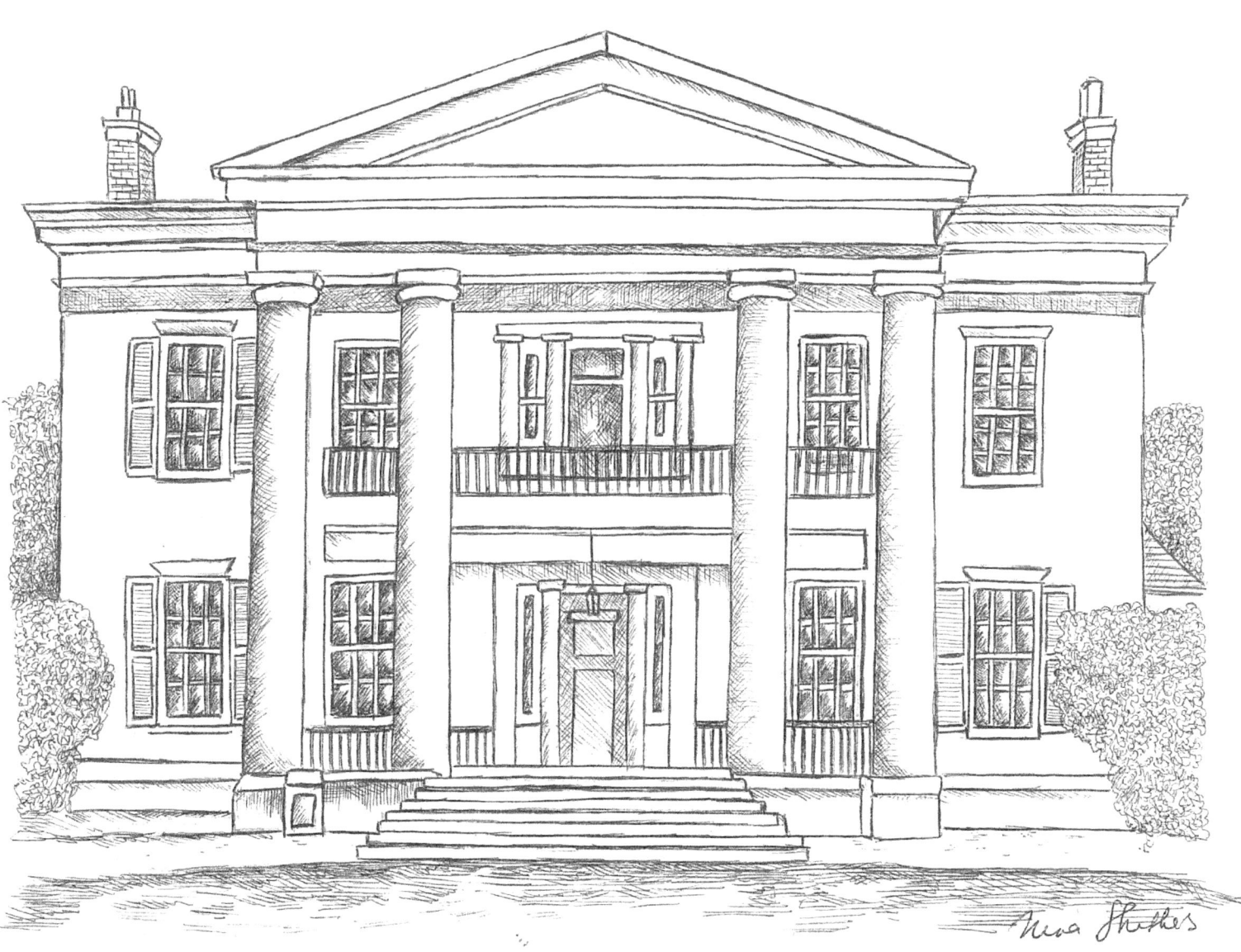

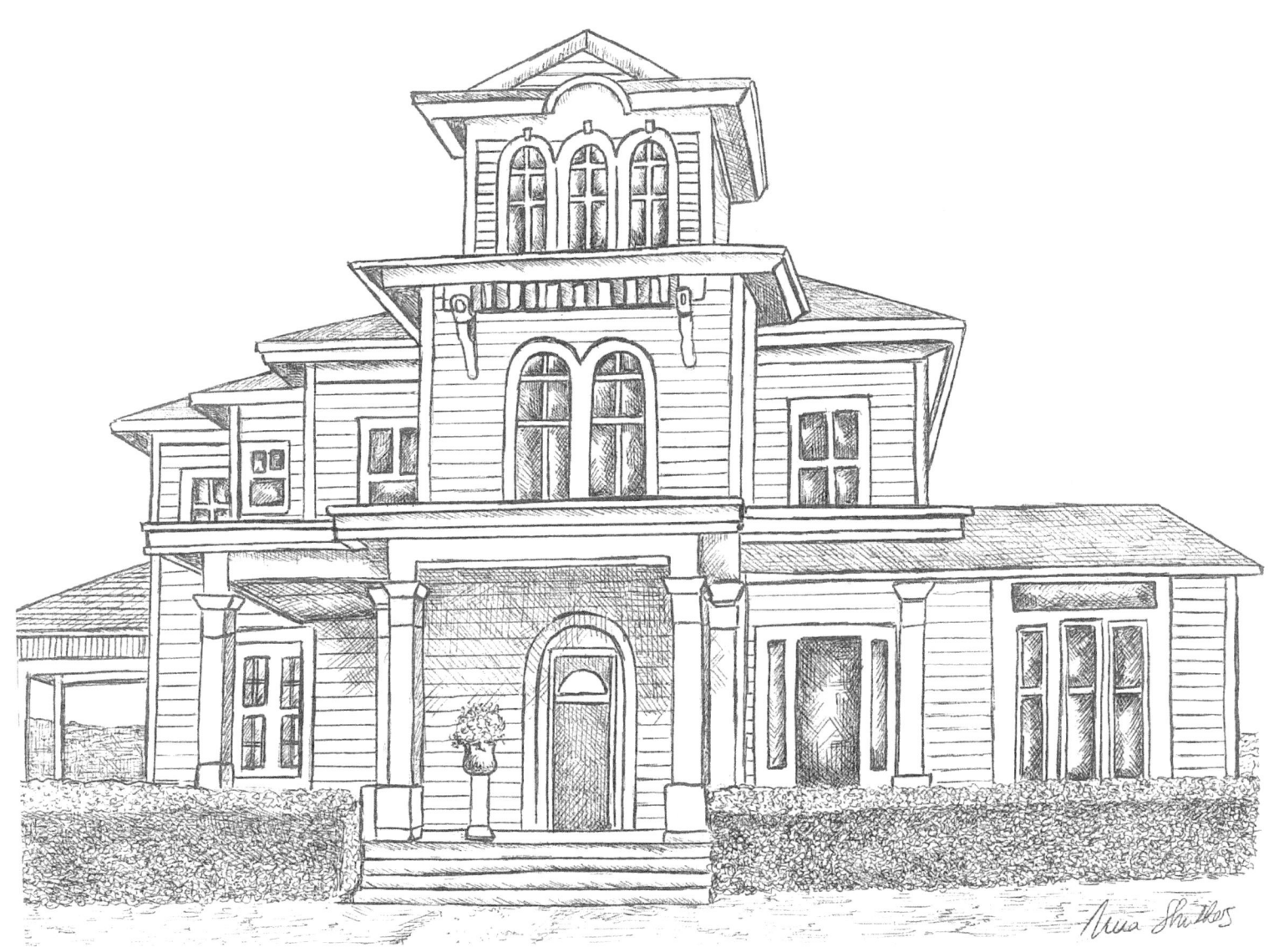

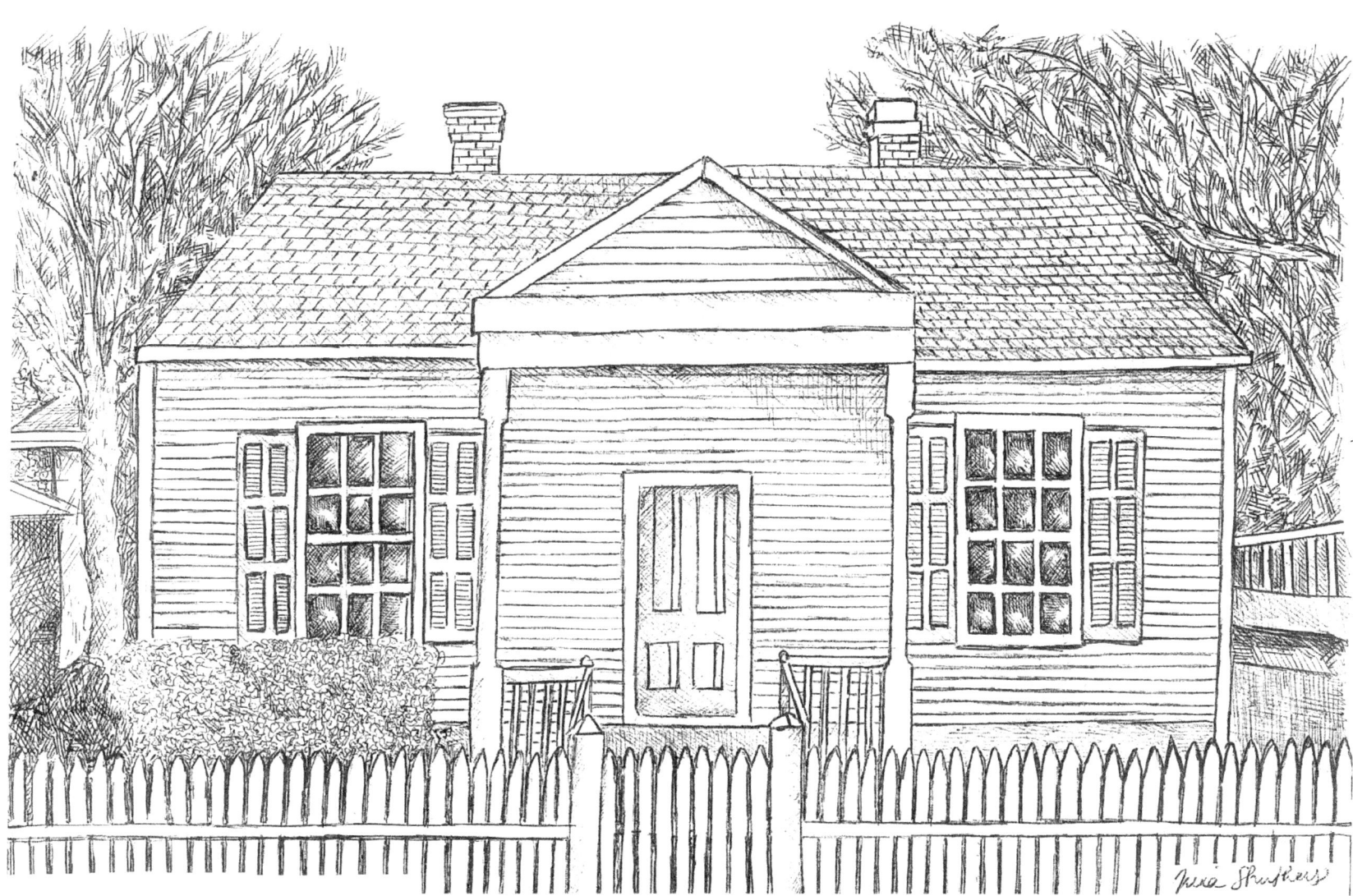

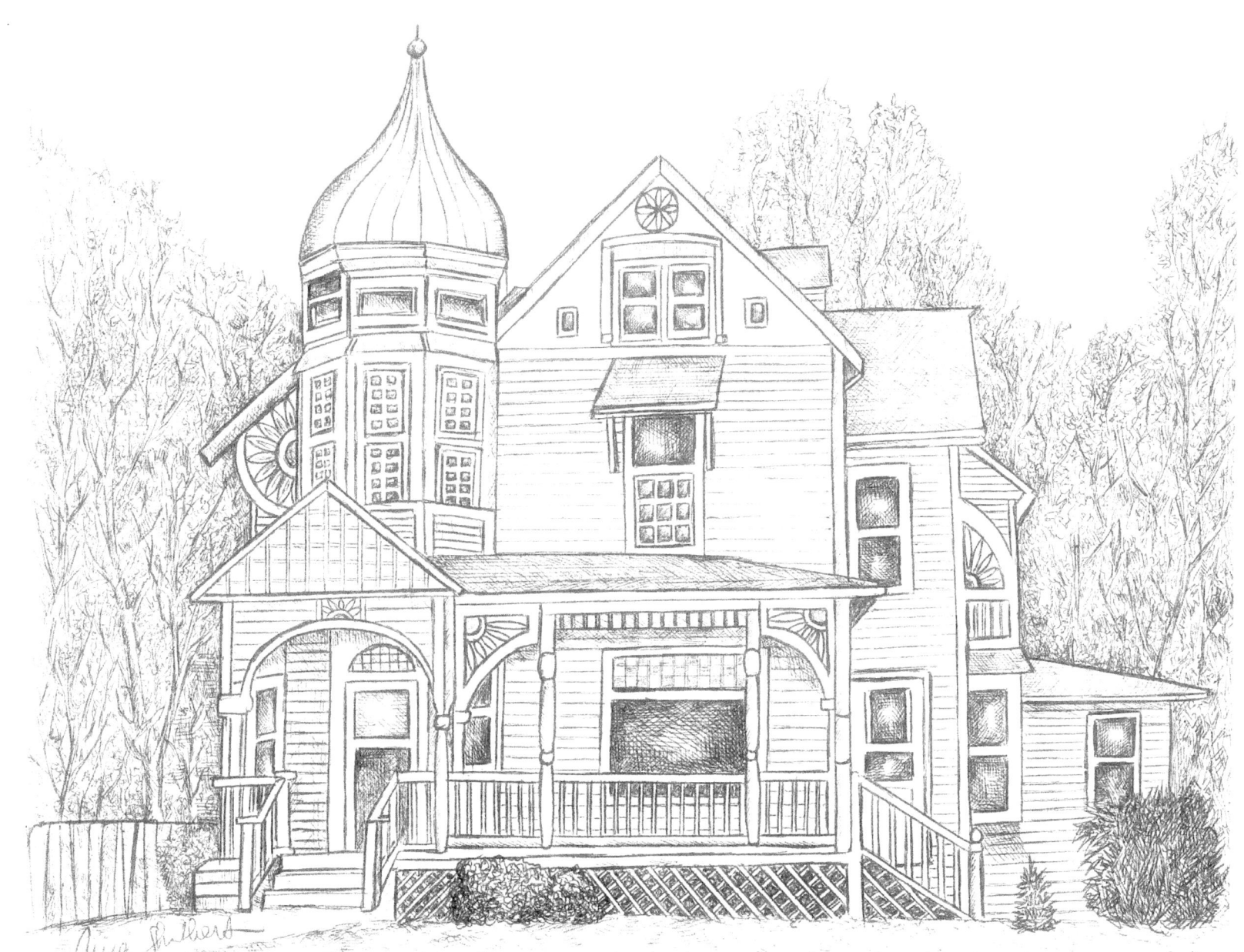

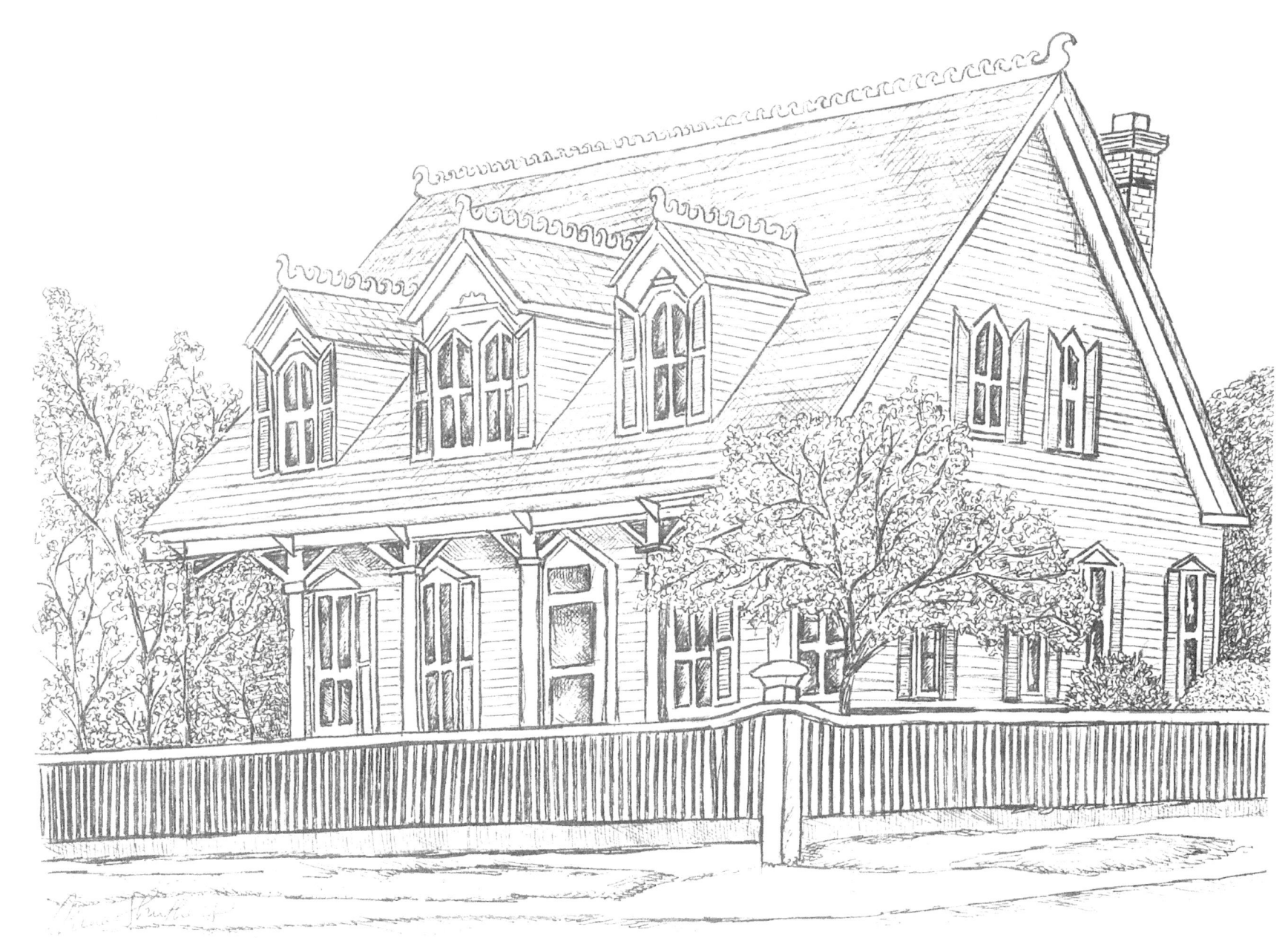

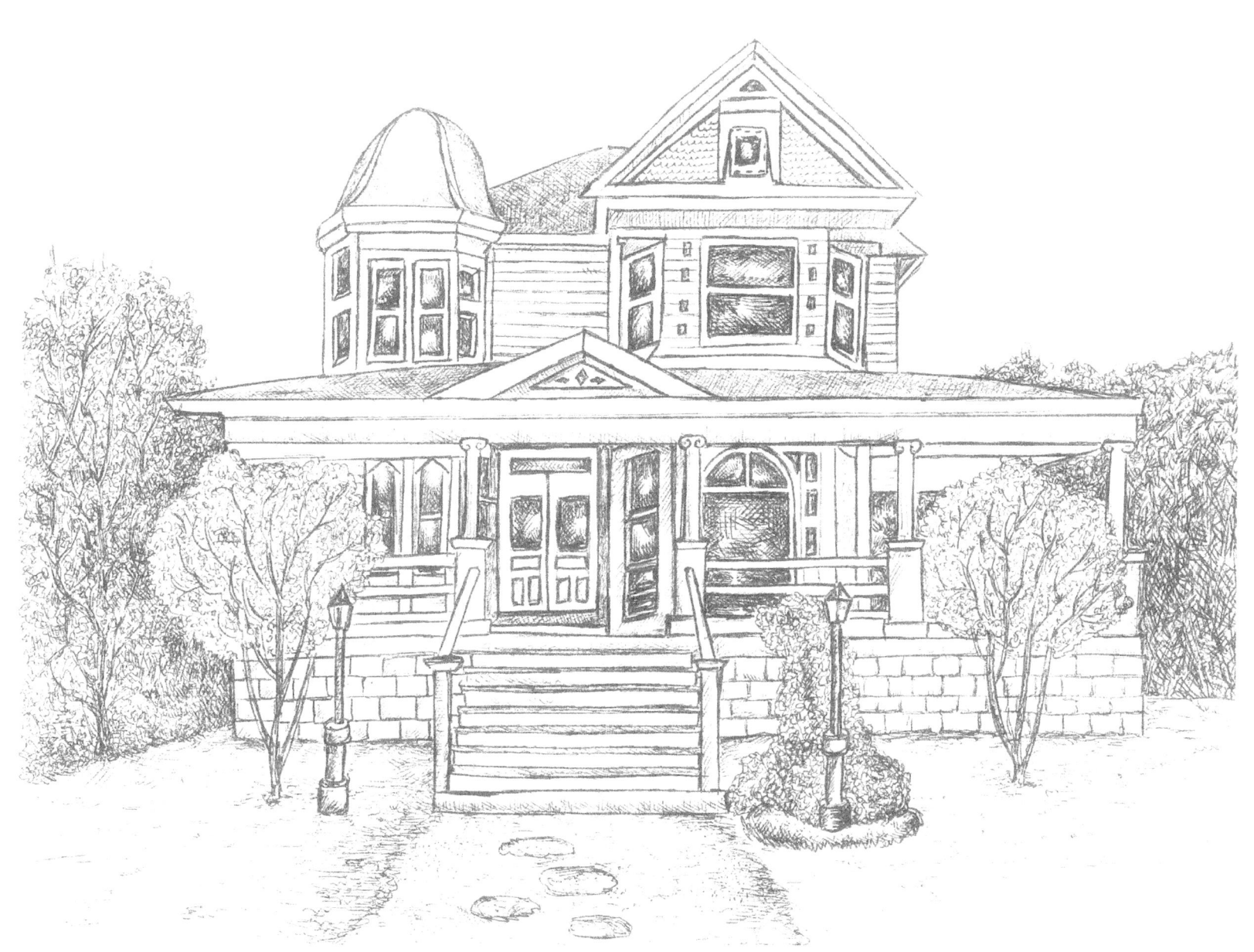

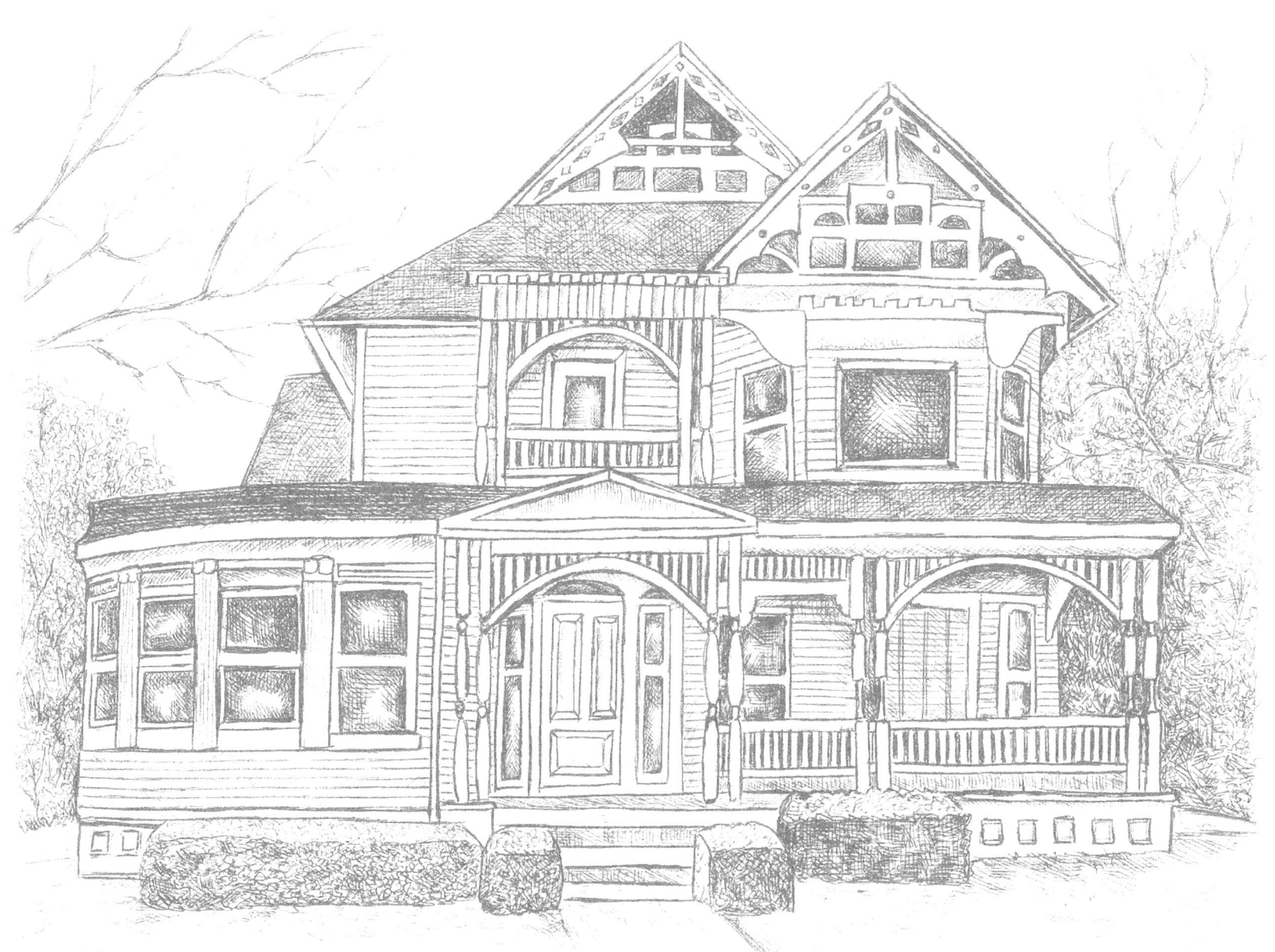

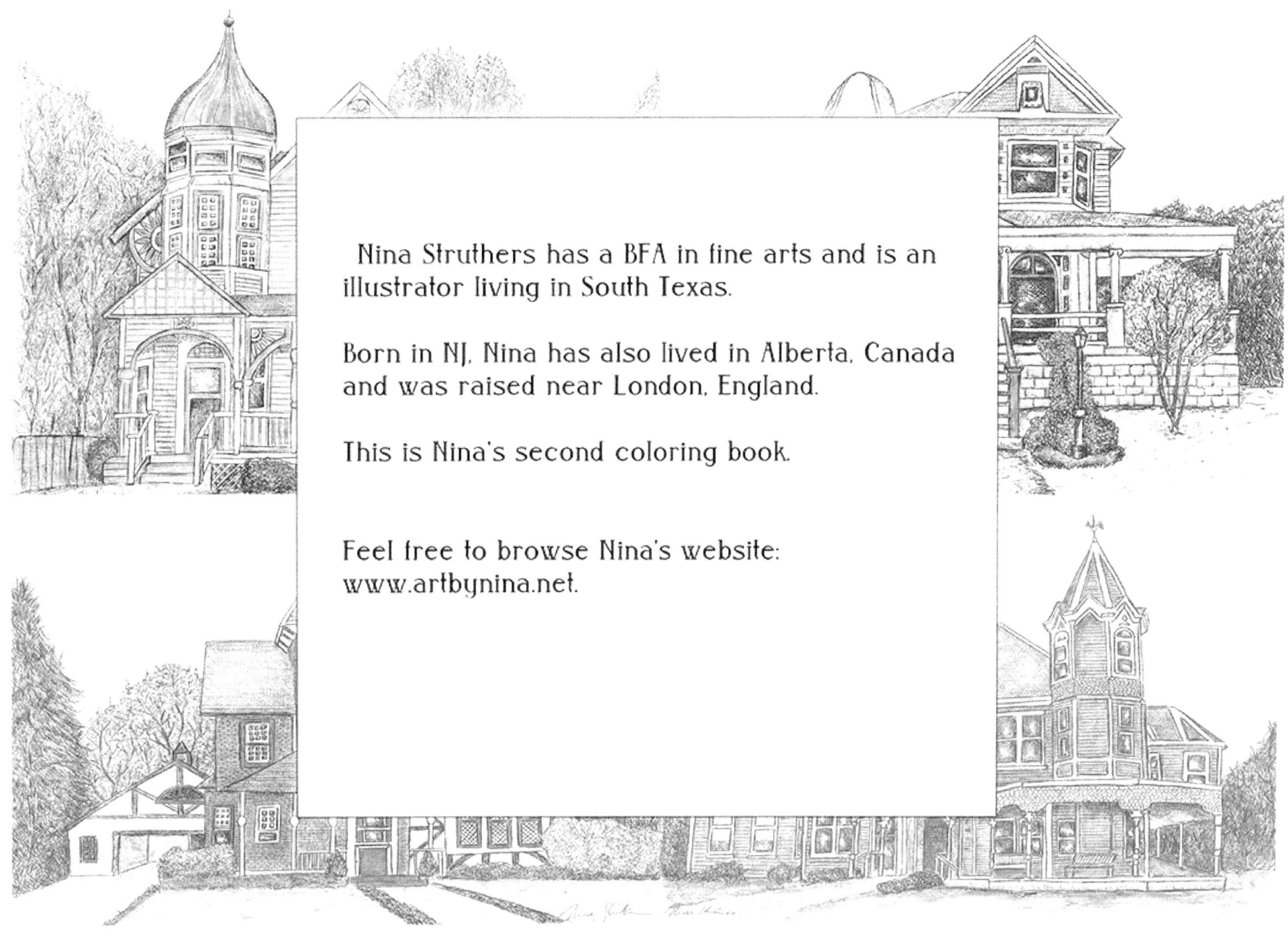

Nina Struthers has a BFA in fine arts and is an illustrator living in South Texas.

Born in NJ, Nina has also lived in Alberta, Canada and was raised near London, England.

This is Nina's second coloring book.

Feel free to browse Nina's website: www.artbynina.net.